An AMERICAN JOURNEY of TRAVELS and FRIENDSHIPS

GEORGE WILLIAM "BILL" PERKINS, II
WITH
KAREN L. GIBSON

AN AMERICAN JOURNEY OF TRAVELS AND FRIENDSHIPS

iUniverse books may be ordered through booksellers or by contacting:

iUniverse
1663 Liberty Drive
Bloomington, IN 47403
www.iuniverse.com
1-800-Authors (1-800-288-4677)

Because of the dynamic nature of the Internet, any web addresses or links contained in this book may have changed since publication and may no longer be valid. The views expressed in this work are solely those of the author and do not necessarily reflect the views of the publisher, and the publisher hereby disclaims any responsibility for them.

Any people depicted in stock imagery provided by Getty Images are models, and such images are being used for illustrative purposes only.
Certain stock imagery © Getty Images.

ISBN: 978-1-5320-6805-8 (sc)
ISBN: 978-1-5320-6806-5 (e)

Library of Congress Control Number: 2019920036

Print information available on the last page.

iUniverse rev. date: 12/16/2019

Dear Mildred,

This is my invitation to enjoy our annual dinner at the Colonial Inn in Concord, Massachusetts where we spent our first night and day after our wedding on October 6, 1951. We have been *dedicated* to each other ever since and deeply in love.

Your Husband!
Bill

To live in hearts
We leave behind
Is not to die.
Thomas Campbell

I met Robert Bouchier as a student sitting in my classroom at Curry College while I was teaching there in the nineteen sixties. He was attentive and interested in class. He helped set the "learning stage". After his graduation we remained friends and his new wife, Sue, joined in the friendship. Christmas cards helped us. They lived in California while I continued to live in the Boston area.

Sadly, Robert was taken from us in 2016. Sue has remained my distant friend whom I cherish. The notice of his loss came to me by mail. Its message was the Thomas Campbell quote above. The words are so thoughtful and meaningful that they have a permanent place in my valued memories. Thank you, Sue.

PREFACE

Hi, and welcome! I am delighted to have this opportunity to tell you about my memories of special people who have helped guide my life. The most exceptional person of all has to have been my dad. He understood what life was all about. I grew up watching Dad's friendships last forever, and through the years I witnessed the true meaning of having long-term friendships. I observed that my dad was his happiest when he was enjoying the companionship of others. While witnessing his fellowship with special people, I learned that cultivating new friendships is an important part of living a happy life.

I enjoy having a book that can be picked up and opened to any page for the enjoyment of quick and interesting short stories on many different subjects. I look forward to your reading my true short stories about my friends, my memories, and my exciting, love-filled life.

PROLOGUE

What makes life worth living? My simple answer is "special people", and I am the living proof of it. Life is much too dear to waste even a moment being negative. Life tends to be what we encourage it to be as we live it day by day. I think of my life as unique, that it must be well used.

I am overwhelmed as I relive some of the moments that seemed so simple but demanded instant activity, such as the adventure of driving what was at the time the world's smallest 4-door automobile, the Renault 4CV, on the Alaskan Highway. I am remembering how important special people were who gave me the opportunities to try to be like them. The greatest moments in my life were with those people. I plan to honor them by writing about them.

This book is a collection of the voices and actions of others that together have made me into the man I am. It tends to remind me of the right decisions, and of the many errors I failed to avoid. Writing this book is almost like living my life a second time. I'm learning what to write about, such as the first Dude Ranch, and the 600-pound red hog that floated down the Merrimack River in a storm.

I learned a good lesson in a story I read years ago. One stormy night, an elderly man and his wife entered the lobby of a small hotel in Philadelphia. The couple had no luggage. "All the big places are filled up," said the man. "Can you possibly give us a room here?"

The clerk replied that there were three conventions in town and no accommodations anywhere. "Every guest room is taken," he next explained. "But still I simply can't send a nice couple like you out in the rain at 1 o'clock in the morning. Would you perhaps be willing to sleep in my room?"..."I'll make out just fine; don't worry about me."

Next morning as he paid his bill the elderly man said to the clerk, "You are the kind of manager who should be boss of the best hotel in the United States. Maybe some day I'll build one for you." The clerk laughed. And he laughed again when after two years had passed he received a letter containing a round-trip ticket to New York and a request that he call upon his guest of that rainy night. In the metropolis, the old man led the young clerk to the corner of 5th Avenue and 34th Street and pointed to a vast new building, a palace of reddish stone with turrets and watchtowers, like a castle from fairyland cleaving the New York sky. "That," he declared, "is the hotel I have just built for you to manage."

As if hit by lightning, the young man, George C. Boldt, stood fixed to the ground. His benefactor was William Waldorf Astor, and the hotel, the most famous of its day, the original Waldorf-Astoria.

CONTENTS

MEETING DICK RANDALL

1

Dad was an active member of the Hotel Greeters Association of Boston. He was a large man at six feet in height and about 240 pounds of muscle (from his railroading days). He was very careful about his appearance and never left his home on a workday without freshly shined shoes.

Dad's laugh and smile served him well and made people want to be around him. His thundering laugh was infectious and could be heard from a considerable distance. If you heard it once, you recognized and remembered it all your life; that laugh told you he was nearby, even if you couldn't see him. People of all ages and backgrounds—men and women alike—were drawn to him. His warm and welcoming smile made him many friends, and he always shared his friends with his family. One such person to be drawn to Dad's smile was James Norris Randall.

"Dick," as he preferred to be called, was a slender man of medium height, but to me, he had an imposing stature. His thinning white hair and wrinkled face betrayed the fact that he was hardened at sixty-four years old. The thing that made him perfect and made me almost numb with admiration for him was that he was a cowboy—a true cowboy. I was only four years old, but I had been studying to be a cowboy my entire life.

Dick came to Boston to promote his large dude ranch, called the OTO, located in Cedar Creek, Montana. He had welcomed a great many visitors from Europe to his ranch, which could accommodate over one hundred guests at a time. All guests were called *dudes*, primarily because they were so dressed up when they arrived, but most of the guests started wearing ranch-type clothing very quickly.

Dick had been traveling for many days when my dad met him. This was in 1930, when most people traveled by train or bus to get to their destinations. Dad invited Dick to have a home-cooked dinner with us, and his invitation was gratefully accepted by the weary traveler. I was witness that evening to the beginning of one of Dad's enduring friendships, one that would continue for as long as my dad was alive.

When Dad arrived home that evening and introduced Dick to me, I was instantly filled with excitement. Dick was wearing a fringed deerskin coat, a ten-gallon Stetson hat, a large polished silver-and-gold belt buckle, and cowboy boots with two-inch heels. Here in my very own home was a real live cowboy, sitting right beside me! I was just four years old, and I was totally wowed.

I told Dick how much I needed a grandfather. My young friends all had at least one grandfather, but both of mine had died before I was born. Dick put his hand on top of mine and said, "Bill, we're partners now." (We were partners in his world, but in mine he was always to be my grandfather.) "Your dad is planning to come to see me at my ranch, and I have invited you and your mother to come with him."

After dinner, he and Dad talked for a long time. My mother knew how excited I was to be with a cowboy. She let me stay up longer than I ever had. Just before I went to bed, Dick said to me, "Bill, when your family comes to my ranch, I'll have your own horse all saddled and ready to ride. My daughter, Bess, is a wonderful rider, and she will teach you to ride your horse just like the cowboys do. Bill, this is a promise. Whenever you make a promise, you have to be sure to keep it. That's the way we live at our ranch. It is a part of the western way. When you make a promise, you shake hands to seal your promise. Let me shake your hand. I have made you my promise." It was the first time I had ever shaken the hand of a man and a real cowboy. Wow!

That night I learned about promises, and it served me well. It began my education on how to live with many different people. I would see how some people can be careless in living up to the promises they make; their promises are just words. I became conscious of that fact.

I have tried to keep all my promises. The biggest promise I ever made was to Mildred, when she agreed to marry me. That promise is sacred to me and has never been broken, all because of Dick. Thank you, Dick.

COMPARING SNAKES

2

Dick Randall and Dad talked about their lives and previous work, of Panama and Costa Rica, Yellowstone National Park and Big Sky Country. Dad commented that in Central America, snakes were a bit of a problem, and Dick told Dad that Montana had its share of rattlesnakes that could grow to be fairly large.

Dick was interested in the snakes. Dad went down into our basement and brought up a couple of snakeskins he kept there. One was eight feet long, and the other was eleven feet long. Dick was delighted.

"What are you going to do with the skins?" Dick asked Dad.

Dad said to him, "Dick, if you had them, what would you do with them?"

"I'd tack them up on the wall in the big room at the ranch, where all of my guests congregate," Dick answered. "I'd tell my guests, 'We have good-sized snakes here in Montana. You all have your own horses, and you are able to ride anywhere you please. I would suggest that you stay out of that little canyon you pass every day. We have seen some especially large snakes in there.'"

This was all true and tended to be exciting for someone from London or Berlin. Most of the "dudes" stayed away from the little canyon.

My dad said to Dick—and for some reason I can see it in my memory as clearly as if it was yesterday — "They are yours."

"How much do I owe you, George?" Dick asked.

"Not a dime," Dad replied. "Giving them to you and knowing the fun you will have with them makes me a happy man. I have your address; I'll ship them to you tomorrow."

Dad shared with Dick that he looked forward to a great friendship between their two families. That night, Dad said to me, "I want to show you the western states, and we will visit the Randall family when we do."

"Grandfather" Randall's influence on me continued. I was really lucky because he and Dad found time to be together often, and they both decided I could be with them whenever they talked. Dad wanted to know more about Dick and how he had achieved so much. Dick seemed eager to let his white hair down and really talk about his life, and I believe he trusted the advice he got from Dad.

Dad wrote a lot of notes about Dick's stories, giving precious details. He kept those notes, and later, I saved them. My dad's written notes have helped me to recall so much, including that first meeting with the Randalls, folks who would forever change the way I wished to live my life. I have a very good memory, though, and that first evening supper with the stranger, soon to become Grandfather, still stands out in my mind so clearly.

DAD AND DICK RANDALL— THE COMPARISON

3

Comparing my dad to my adopted grandfather, Dick Randall, surprised me. They were two men from another century with broad similarities. I am filled with respect for both of these remarkable, family-oriented, honest, diligent, and progressive individuals.

Both of these men created opportunities that benefited many people, including me. I give my thanks to both my dad and my adopted grandfather for being kind men.

- Dad was born in 1875; Dick was born in 1866.
- Dad didn't attend college; neither did Dick, Dad's early work included pushing railroad freight cars by hand; Dick became a cowboy at age eighteen.
- Dad and Dick both engaged in very hard work and enjoyed it.
- For both men, their work also was very dangerous at times.
- Both were interested in snakes.
- Both men were happily married.
- Dad had just one child; Dick had two children.
- When they met each other, Dad was fifty-five years old, and Dick was sixty-four.
- Dad owned a hotel; Dick owned a ranch-type hotel.
- Dad's stories were good; Dick's stories were huge.
- Both men traveled often.
- Both men had great courage.

OTO DUDE RANCH

4

My adopted grandfather was a fascinating storyteller. All you needed to do was sit comfortably, relax, perhaps ask a question, be patient, and wait for his thoughts to enter his memory bank and be converted into spoken words. The result was always more enjoyable and edifying than you could have anticipated.

James Norris "Dick" Randall was born in Ohio in 1866. He left home at age eighteen with nothing but the clothes on his back. Reaching the Montana territory (Montana didn't become a state until 1889), he and another young man of the same age were hired to work for a rancher. They became cowboys.

Once when the rancher needed Dick but couldn't find him, the rancher called out in a loud voice, "Where is that pretty Dick?" The name never left him. He came to

Boston as a judge in the first rodeo in 1932 and was listed on the program as "Judge Pretty Dick Randall." He had to be tough to handle that moniker.

Thousands of cattle were being driven north from Texas. Beef was needed by the army, hotels, and private families. Some of the most important and wealthiest families in Europe were interested in the stories about cowboys and Indians, great herds of bison, and cattle ranging for miles with no fences. The wild game was exciting to the European hunters. Unknown to the ranchers, the changes were setting the stage for the birth of the dude ranch business.

In 1882, the first dude ranch was formed in Wyoming. For the first time, travelers paid to stay overnight at a ranch and take a meal there. There were so many miles between towns at that time that if you were a rancher or even a cowboy, and you needed dinner and a place to sleep, you stopped at the nearest ranch and received both. It was the way in the west.

Dick found that he could do better as a hunter's guide, and he learned how to be an exceptional cook over a campfire. He studied the animals that foreign hunters were seeking. He was ready to be very successful.

Dick was riding through the mountains about twelve miles north of Yellowstone National Park when he met two men who lived in a ramshackle log cabin. The cabin was situated near a creek that came down from the glacier in the high mountains. When Dick learned that the men had been having trouble with the law, he knew it would be wise for them to go where they were not known. He offered to buy their squatter's-rights land and everything on it. The offer was accepted. Now the land was his. His new ranchland was about five thousand acres.

Trapper's Cabin – with 5000 acres
The trapper lived in this windowless cabin with his wife and 5
children. He and his wife slept on the dirt floor and his children
slept in hammocks. The only heat was from a stove.

It was time to settle down, and his now owning the land and the shack of a log cabin was a start. With enormous effort, a new ranch was formed. It would become the OTO Dude Ranch, the first dude ranch in the state of Montana. Dick looked out his window and saw two wagon wheels separated by a drag bar in the shape of a "T". That was the inspiration for naming it the OTO Ranch. It was all Dick's idea, and it was destined to become world famous, attracting English royalty, wealthy German families like the Von Hindenburgs, and Theodore Roosevelt and his family.

Dick was a very good shot with his pistols. He would put tin cans up on fence posts along the ranch road on his way to pick up guests at the railroad station in his wagon. On the way back, riding his horse, he would shoot the cans off the posts. He had a great reputation as a gunslinger. I was twenty-nine years old before he told me he was using .44-caliber shells loaded with birdshot! He was a great character.

Yellowstone National Park became the first national park in the world in 1872. It was very dear to the heart of President Theodore Roosevelt, who had hunted that entire area with Dick Randall as his guide. In 1903, President Roosevelt spoke at the dedication ceremony for the fifty-foot-high Roosevelt Arch at the northern entrance to the park, but he refused to begin until Dick Randall was found and rushed to sit on the speaker's platform.

Bess Randall Erskine, Dick's daughter, told me when I was twenty-nine years old the reason her dad was late to the dedication ceremony, holding up President Roosevelt's speech. Dick had been helping their next-door neighbor, a woman named Martha Jane Canary, deliver milk to the young children in town. Canary, better known as Calamity Jane, really needed Dick's help because she was intoxicated. Calamity Jane was famous as an army Indian scout and the only woman scout in the country. She was a tough lady among tough men, but she had a kind side that was seldom remembered. She enjoyed the Randall children.

The wealthy and titled English nobles who were guests of the OTO called Dick "Governor." The name had glue upon it because for the rest of Dick's life, he was often referred to as "Governor."

Original Brochure for the OTO Dude Ranch 1919
Dick Randall on the horse

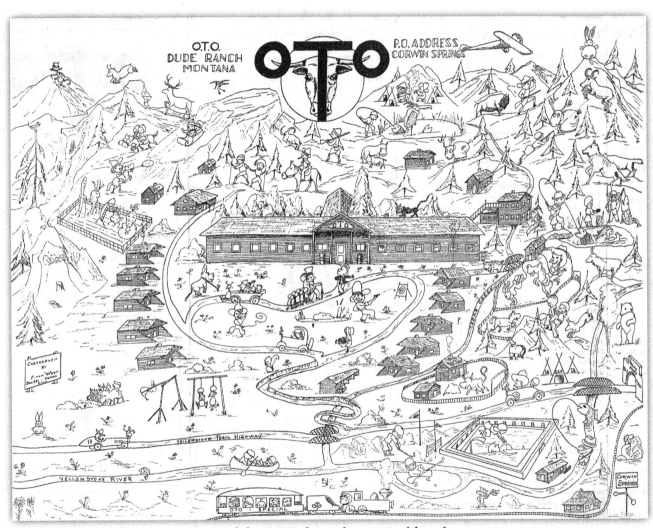

Map of the OTO from the original brochure

An American Journey of Travels and Friendships

Rates and Offerings from the Original Brochure
$90 per week =

Rates at the Ranch

The rates, from $45 to $90 per week (payable by cash or traveler's check only), are given on the American Plan, with the exclusive use of a saddle-horse. (There are 200 fine looking, gentle horses.) Riding lessons and guides for daily trips are free.

In order to insure accommodations, advance reservations are necessary, and should be accompanied by a 20 per cent deposit on the period reserved. Season June 20th to September 1st. A post office is on the ranch, western garb may be purchased.

Auto meets guests by appointment.

References exchanged.

Trout Stream Runs by the Door

What the O T O Ranch Vacation Offers You

The O T O Ranch is an old frontier cattle ranch, where, amid western romance and in the heart of the old historic west, you can ride, hike, climb mountains, fish, hunt or rest and enjoy vigorous pastime or lazy enjoyment in whatever degree you wish, and enjoy life in a natural setting of rare beauty. New health and energy await you here on your vacation that is different.

Historical Background

Nestled in a picturesque spot and surrounded by snow-capped mountains and the Absaroka National Forest. In the famous Indian hunting grounds, famous also because of the Lewis & Clack Expedition in 1806. We are located in the south-western corner of Montana, amid lakes and pure mountain streams with Yellowstone Park just next door.

Climate and Altitude

Bright days of sunshine. Cool nights of rest. One mile above sea level. Where the air is fresh and pure, laden with the scent of pine and sage.

Railroad and Highway

4½ miles from Corwin Springs station on the Yellowstone Park line of the Northern Pacific Ry. Ranch cars meet trains by appointment.

2 miles via ranch private road from Yellowstone Trail Highway.

50 miles from Livingston. 12 miles from Gardiner. 60 miles from West Yellowstone Union Pacific Ry. entrance to the Park.

Mail - Telegraph - Express

P. O. address, Dude Ranch, Montana. Mail daily except Sunday. Post office at Ranch. Express and Railway station, Corwin Springs. Telegraph via Livingston, Montana.

Buildings

Comfortable rustic log buildings accommodating 75 guests offering every convenience and a home-like atmosphere.

All rooms are comfortably furnished, electrically lighted throughout and good beds. Rooms in main lodge with bath. Individual cabins with detached showers. Dining room in main lodge. Large living room and recreation room and den with large fireplaces.

Food and Supplies

The best and purest of food is served family style. Pure ice cold water from a mountain stream. Fresh vegetables from our own gardens. Fresh rich milk and cream, butter, and buttermilk are supplied by our own dairy herd of tested registered Guernsey cows. Choice beef from our own herds. Poultry and eggs. Fresh fruits are supplied from the Pacific Coast. And you will agree that our Chef is a wonder.

Horses

An experienced wrangler assigns each guest a good horse according to the individual's experience and riding ability. From the cavvy herd of more than 200 good saddle horses there are plenty of gentle, reliable, trail-wise mounts for the children and beginners. Free expert riding instruction (if desired) and guide service for day trips.

Pack, Hunting and Fishing Trips

Pack trips with licensed guides may be arranged in advance for hunting trips or fishing trips to the back country. There is splendid fishing in all the streams and lakes near the ranch. Excellent hunting from Ranch in season. A copy of game laws will be mailed upon request. Licenses may be secured at the ranch.

Laundry

This work is done at the Ranch at current rates.

Medical Aid

The best sanitariums, hospital, and physicians can be reached within an hour's drive or less by auto from the Ranch.

Commissary - Store

A small commissary is maintained at the Ranch for your convenience. Anything not carried in stock may be obtained within 24 hours.

Recreations

HORSE-BACK RIDING
MOUNTAIN CLIMBING
HUNTING, FISHING
RODEO, JULY 2-3-4
PACK TRAIN TRIPS

Regular Ranch Activities and Sports
Golf and Swimming Pool at Corwin Springs

For further information, rates, reservation, etc., address—

Manager, O T O Ranch
Dude Ranch, Montana

OTO Lodge made from over 1000 hand cut logs

Foot pedestal of the billiard table – gift from the King of Prussia

Martha Jane Canary AKA Calamity Jane

First Rodeo in the East

Rodeo Officials

MILT HINKLE (the South American Kid)
Director-General

GEORGE SWARTZ
Executive Director

E. M. JACOBS
Exclusive Booking Representative

HORTON W. CAMPBELL
Secretary

RENE BELAIRE
Adjuster

MILT HINKLE
Arena Director

JACK F. MURRAY
Publicity Director

"TEXAS" JACK SULLIVAN
Special Exploitation

R. L. GORMAN
Supt., Admissions

SHORTY RICKER
Supt., Stock, Steer Riding and Wrestling Division

FRED BRISTOW
Supt., Stock, Bronk Riding Division

GRADY WILSON
Supt., Chutes and Corrals

LLOYD SCHERMERHORN
Supt., Fancy Roping and Trick Riding Events

BRONCHO JOHN SULLIVAN
Supt., Prairie Schooners and Western Exhibits

CLYDE MILLER
Supt., Jumping Events

FOG HORN CLANCY
Official Announcer

TEX COOPER
Assistant Announcer

Judges
BILLY BINDER - - CANDY HAMMER
AUVIL GILLIAM - - PRETTY DICK RANDALL

Pretty Dick Randall – Rodeo Judge

1932 Rodeo Dictionary for First Rodeo in the East

RODEO DICTIONARY

THE RODEO and the West have their own dictionary. As Western life continued, as the Rodeo was more widely developed, terms of the range came into more popular use. But even some of the Rodeo fans do not know the dictionary of the cowboy.

A cowboy dictionary follows:

BICYCLING—The act of scratching with first one foot and then the other in the manner of riding a bicycle.

BITING THE DUST—Being thrown from a horse.

BLOWING A STIRRUP—Losing a stirrup, which disqualifies rider.

BOGGING THEM IN—When rider fails to scratch horse.

BRONCO—Mexican word for "mean," shortened to "bronc or bronk," in cowboy parlance, a vicious, unbroken horse.

BROOMTAIL—Wild mares.

BRONC-BUSTER—Cowboy who "breaks" broncs.

BUCKAROO—Cowboy.

BUCKING, BUCK-JUMPING, PITCHING—The gyrations of a bronc trying to unseat rider.

BULLDOGGING—Often termed steer wrestling; the throwing of a steer by his horns in a Rodeo event, subject to rules of the contest.

BULL-DOGGER—A steer wrestler.

CANTLE-BOARDING—When rider scratches back to cantle.

CAVY or REMUDA—Saddle horses on a Round-up.

CHAPS—The leather or hair leggings worn by the cowboy to protect his limbs from the thorns or from rain.

CHUCK WAGON—The rangeland cafeteria which follows the round-up and to which the cowboys come for their meals. The chuck wagon is furnished by the rancher and for days during the rounding up of the herds the cow punchers do not return to the ranch headquarters, but take all their meals at the chuck wagon.

COMMUNITY LOOP—Extra large loop thrown by roper.

CROW-HOPS—A term contemptuously applied to mild bucking motions.

CUT-OUT—To separate animals from herd.

DOG-FALL—Putting a steer down with its feet under him. The throw is not complete until steer is flat on side with all four feet out.

EATING GRAVEL—Being thrown from a bucking bronc or wild steer.

FOUR FOOTING—Catch an animal by the feet with a rope in order to throw same for handling.

GRABBIN' THE APPLE—When a bronc rider grabs the horn of a saddle to keep from being thrown.

GYPPING—Deceiving.

HAZER—Bull-dogger's assistant. After bull-dogger has leaped from pony to steer, the hazer, mounted, picks up former's mount and also protects him from being gored when he releases steer.

HIGH ROLLER—Horse that leaps high when bucking.

HOBBLED STIRRUPS—Stirrups that are tied down under the horse's belly.

HOOLIHANING—The act of leaping forward and alighting on the horns of a steer in bull-dogging in a manner to knock the steer down without having to resort to twisting the animal down with a wrestling hold. Hoolihaning is barred at practically all recognized contests.

LOSING A STIRRUP—Pulling the foot out of a stirrup while keeping the feet moving in a kicking motion in compliance with contest bronc riding rules. Losing a stirring disqualifies the rider.

MAIL ORDER COWBOY—A tenderfoot in custom-made cowboy regalia and devoid of range experience.

MAN-KILLER—A wild horse with homicidal

mania, that strikes or mounted or unmounted men.

MAVERICK—An unbranded stray; a term well known in the lands of ranches and cattle branding.

NOSE BAG—A canvas receptacle for holding horse feed and which is strapped to the horse's head at feed time, much in the fashion of a halter and from which the horse may eat grain when far away from the feed barn.

OUTFIT—Equipment of ranchmen or Rodeo contestants.

PEGGING—When steer wrestler sticks horn into ground—this is not allowed in bulldogging.

PULLING LEATHER—Holding on to the saddle with the hands while riding a bucking animal, prohibited by the rules of all coontests and scorned by all real cowboys.

RODEO—Pronounced Ro-day-o, with emphasis on second syllable; Mexican word for "Round-Up," or gathering of cattle on open ranges. At round-ups, cowboy contests originated. The World Championship Rodeo is held in Fort Worth each March.

SCRATCHING—The act of keeping the feet moving in a kicking motion in riding buckng anmals, and one of the acts necessary to win at any real contest.

SCREWING DOWN—The act of sinking the spurs into the cinch while riding a bucking horse and failing to move the feet in a kicking motion as provided in the rules.

SEEING DAYLIGHT—When daylight can be seen between rider and saddle during bronc ride.

SOUGAN—A part of the equipment of the cowboys bed and is similar to the ordinary quilt or comforter.

SUN-FISHER—A bucker that twists his body in the aid so that sunlight hits his belly.

TENDERFOOT—That's what you are if you did not know the meaning of these words.

TIGHT LEGGING—When rider holds legs tight against horse and does not scratch.

WALKING-BEAMING—A see-saw motion affected by ingenious buckers, wherein they land alternately on front and hind feet.

WRANGLING—Rounding up, saddling and riding range horses.

In approximately 1920 a producer of a black and white cowboy movie asked Dick Randall if he would ride a horse down the Devil's Slide. Dick had a herd of about 200 horses, but he told the producer that only one might be able to do it. So, he said yes and did it. Afterwards, Dick said it was the stupidest thing he ever did.

PRESIDENT ROOSEVELT AND THE GROTON SCHOOL

5

Mother and Dad knew how important Dick was to four-year-old me. They allowed me to stay up and listen to my dad and Dick talking about their work—the individual tasks caused by their choices of locations, weather, time, and risks. Some of the risks were more than I could understand at the time, but many years later, I realized just how hard it was for my dad and Dick to face those risks and succeed as they did.

What a night it was for a four-year-old—a real live cowboy at dinner, stories, and the invitation to visit a real ranch and learn to ride a horse the way cowboys did. I had a new "pardner" who agreed to become a grandfather by the name of Gramp. To top it all off, that night I learned that we had a Native American in the family. My mother surprised me by telling me that her sister, Mabel, had married Bob Blackbird.

Dick's speaking of his relationship with Theodore Roosevelt brought back memories to my dad. He told Dick about his own experiences with the very same president. Dad's father, William Nathaniel Perkins, born in 1851, became a railroad workman. Dad was born in 1875. He had his first job at age thirteen, lighting the gas lamps on the streets of Nashua, New Hampshire. He had to carry a small step stool in order to reach the lamps. In the blizzard of 1888, the snow was so deep that Dad could walk up the drifts to reach the lamps, so he left his step stool at home.

At the age of sixteen, Dad rented canoes on the Nashua River. He found great pleasure in working very hard. As soon as he was old enough, his dad helped him join the railroad. His work attitude helped him to become a freight handler very quickly. He was strong and weighed about 240 pounds, and he needed all of his strength. Freight handlers had to push freight cars by hand when loading and unloading. Dad spent a short time in freight. He quickly became a trainman and then a conductor. Passengers enjoyed interacting with him.

President Roosevelt's son, Theodore Jr., was a student at the famous Groton School in Groton, Massachusetts. While there, he became very sick. The president came to Nashua, and from there, he took a train to Groton. Dad was chosen to act as the conductor on that train. He and "Teddy" really hit it off. They became friends, and their genuine friendship lasted until Teddy died. Dad said that Teddy asked him to let him know if the train passed by people—the population at the time was very small—so that he could wave to them.

When Teddy Jr. recovered from his illness, the president returned to Washington. It was on this train trip that Dad first learned about Alice, the president's oldest child, who was already very blunt and independent.

In 1907, the Panama Canal still was unfinished. It was a colossal project. In order to complete it, many more men were needed. The French I am told started the project, lost over five thousand men because of malaria, yellow fever, and the general conditions under which they worked. Dad had an offer to sign up for a year as experienced railroad men were needed. The pay was so much better that it was a serious consideration for him. Dad had married Grace Webster in 1897. As they had no children, Grace agreed that the opportunity was too valuable to pass up. She agreed to remain in Nashua and work while Dad was in Panama.

It was a very tough year. Dad found conditions were improved from what he had been told they were, but it was still heavy labor on trains that needed maintenance. Great care was taken to prevent accidents, as medical care was limited.

The United Fruit Company, headquartered in Boston, was involved in raising bananas in both Panama and Costa Rica. They hired Dad when he came home at the end of his year on the canal.

This project was quite different. In a few months, he was able to bring his wife, Grace; his mother and dad; his brother, Harry, and his wife, Delia; and the family dog to Costa Rica. They had a small cottage and endured heat that was quite different from the warm weather in Nashua. Thinking of home, they put a small sign that read NASHUA over their door. They kept a large boa constrictor curled up on their porch, usually under the table that they used for eating. When a stranger would arrive from the United States, they enjoyed leaving the new arrival alone on the porch. There were several times when the new arrivals dashed through the porch door without opening it.

The family stayed for two more years after Dad's first year, when he was alone. The railroad through the banana plantation was narrow-gauge. The trains were small. Snakes were a bit of a problem. The boa constrictors were not venomous, but they grew to a large size. For some reason, they often crawled across the railroad tracks and would stay there on the hot tracks.

Because the trains were small, they could be derailed if the snake refused to move. Dad would leave the train, walk up to the snake, grab it by its tail, and attempt to pull it off the steel tracks. In rare instances, the snakes could be over fifteen feet long and unhappy with his attention. If it refused to move and was too large for him to move it, he sometimes would need to kill the snake. In a few cases, he had the snakeskins cured. They could become good leather.

Teddy Roosevelt in his Rough Rider Gear

RIDE A HORSE LIKE A COWBOY

6

Nine years after Gramp first told me about the importance of keeping one's promises, I learned more about it. In 1939, when I was thirteen, my dad, my mother, and I arrived at the new Randall "JR" Ranch. Dick had told us that the guests who paid to come to the ranch were always dressed in their finest clothes; that's why they were referred to as "dudes." I didn't have any intention of being one of the "dudes"; rather, I was going to be a cowboy!

I dressed as the cowboy I knew I was soon to be. I wore my cowboy jeans, boots, and cowboy hat. We drove down the dirt road to the JR, and in front of a huge horse barn, I saw the most beautiful Paint Horse in the world. Just as promised many years before, the mare was bridled and ready for me. There was even a rifle scabbard attached to the saddle. I couldn't wait to get my gun!

Dressed up and ready to go!

A pretty young woman emerged from the ranch house and ran up to us. She reached out, grabbed my hand, and shook it the way I had learned from Gramp a decade earlier. She held my hand like cowboys do, the way cowboys and cowgirls shake hands when they make their promises to you.

"My name is Bess," she said, "and I'm going to teach you to ride like a cowboy. I can see you're dressed to go, and I'm ready with lesson number one."

Before I could unpack, I was up on that horse. The promise made nine years earlier had been honored and kept! New promises were certain to be on the horizon.

Bess was a wonderful rider and an efficient teacher. At the end of our first week, she exclaimed to everyone, "Billy is ready to ride in his first rodeo parade." She even announced a spectacular surprise. "Bill," she said, "when we're riding in that rodeo parade, our friend Monty Montana will be riding along with us."

Monty Montana was a famous horseman of significant reputation, and it impressed everyone that each year he rode in the Annual Rose Parade in Pasadena, California. It was said that Monty Montana was the only man who had ever performed the "Four-Rider Lasso"—he was able to rope and bring down four riders, astride their horses, with a single throw of the lasso. The fact he was also a friend of the Randalls made him a proper hero to me.

Bess, Monty, and I rode beside one another in the Livingston Montana Rodeo Parade of 1939. It was exciting for me, at age thirteen, to have a girlfriend who was twenty years older than me and to be the friend of a famous cowboy hero. It should always be remembered that kept promises make little boys' dreams come true.

I continued a warm and loving relationship with Bess and her husband, Clyde, as they made hotel history in Yellowstone National Park; Death Valley; Phoenix, Arizona; Boulder, Colorado; Lake Mead; and the Hoover Dam by creating exceptional new hotel construction and management. When I was sixty and Bess was about eighty, I wrote her a note:

> Bess, Bess, with your eyes so blue,
> When I was thirteen, I fell in love with you.
> Now that I am sixty, nothing has changed.
> I am always so happy when we are together again.

The family friendship between the Randalls and Perkinses is still strong, even though most of the older members are gone.

Box Camera photo of Dick Randall, George
II, Bess Erskine and Clyde Erskine

SWIMMING IN YELLOWSTONE

7

In 1939, Dad, Mother, and I spent several days with Dick and Dora Randall on their new JR Ranch in Livingston, Montana, located on a mile-long edge of the Yellowstone River, one of the rare long rivers in the United States that has no dams. I still had so much to learn about ranch life and the way everything had to be done.

Dick's wife, who asked me to call her Aunt Dora, said to me, "What would you like for supper?"

At age thirteen, I had trouble answering because we had just arrived that day.

She said, "Do you like fried chicken?" I did like it and told her so. She said, "Come with me."

I followed her out the kitchen door and found a fenced area with many chickens eating and walking about. She leaned down and grabbed the first chicken she could catch. She was very practiced. With her right hand she reached over and picked up a small hatchet and with a single swing, she removed the chicken's head. In five minutes she had four headless chickens running about, spurting blood. I had never seen anything like that and was nearly speechless and in shock over the blood and the headless chickens. I had been introduced to the life of a ranch woman who had no supermarkets.

In just about an hour, the chickens had been stripped of their feathers, cleaned, and cut up properly and were frying. I, in turn, wondered if I could eat them so soon after the execution. I also wondered what the next two weeks would hold in my education of ranch living way out west.

While there, I observed their grandson, Bill Randall, applying gorgeous leather decorations on a new saddle. He showed a belt to me that was a true work of art. I knew I wanted to do something like it myself. When our trip ended and we were back in our Melrose, Massachusetts home, I decided to try to make a western-style belt for my dad. I bought the tools and did my best. It was a first try, not perfect but very wearable and much appreciated by my dad. Today, I enjoy "his" belt almost every day and the joyful memories of Dick, Dora, Bess, Bill, and everything that has been created by our lifetime of friendship.

This morning when I pulled on a pair of jeans and reached for a belt, my hand caught the brown leather western-style belt I made for my dad in 1946. Memories of so many things came rushing to me. Like my dad, friendships have come effortlessly to me.

Yellowstone Park was about forty miles away from the ranch. As I've mentioned, Yellowstone was the first national park in the world, and it was my very own adopted grandfather Dick who stood beside President Roosevelt when the dedication ribbons were cut. I had dreamed of traveling there.

Dick mentioned that the Geyser Water Swimming Pool at Old Faithful geyser was open. When the geyser's water was blown out of the ground, it was channeled into the pool. Dad and Mother had no interest in swimming in the geyser water, but I thought it was a great idea.

We drove to the park, followed the signs to the Old Faithful geyser, and found the pool facility. Many people were watching the great sight of that powerful geyser as it blew its hot water very high in the air. As soon as that activity was over, we went directly to the pool.

Only a couple of other cars were there. The park, even in 1939, drew large numbers of visitors, so we were surprised. We went inside and found a very nice pool that was well maintained and empty of any swimmers. I was delighted. I was wearing my bathing suit under my clothes, so I hastened to take off my shirt and pants and enter the pool. Instantly, I knew why no one else was in that runoff of geyser water! *It was so hot!* I could stand it but not for long! I was glad that Mother took my picture in the few minutes I was in it. The pool was closed in 1951.

FORTY-EIGHT STATES

8

Dad came home from the office one day and told Mother that he wanted to be sure that I had been in all forty-eight of the United States before my graduation from high school. (Alaska and Hawaii were not states until a number of years later.) He believed in travel as a major contributor to a person's education. Dad never smoked. He told Mother that he had been putting a nickel in a different pocket every time anyone in his carpool smoked a cigar. He had been doing it for three years. He told her he had saved enough money to travel for two months and had the accumulated free time at work.

They laid out the travel plan to cover as many states as possible. We would travel during all of July and August. In the summer of 1939, I was twelve years old, turning thirteen in September. It was a major trip by car and would turn out to be the year that I was able to ride in my first rodeo parade and attend the New York World's Fair when the King George VI and Queen Elizabeth of England were there.

Many gas stations would advertise low gas prices in competition with other stations in the same area. There were times when we were able to buy ten gallons of gas for a dollar. Dad loved to drive. There were very few roads similar to what we have now. Driving 250 miles was a long day, as most roads were designed for speeds of thirty-five to forty miles per hour.

This trip would include a visit to the Squilaris, who had bought our hotel years before; a visit with an old school friend of Mother's in San Francisco; several days at the Randall Ranch in Montana—time to hunt prairie dogs, crows, and some of the black and white birds that were stealing Aunt Dora's chicks; a visit to Yellowstone Park and fishing for trout in its river; and a long list of other places.

THE BIRTH OF GEORGE PERKINS

9

The most incredible thing that could ever happen to me occurred at two minutes past noon on Friday, September 10, 1926, in Salem, Massachusetts. I was born! One year later, on September 10, 1927, I received my first birthday gift from Frederick Snyder.

Frederick owned a business, and my dad had been his best salesman for several years. They became lifelong friends. This remarkably wonderful man gave his friendship to me as well. For my first birthday, he sent me his own Boy Scout jackknife with a note telling me that I must use it carefully when I was old enough to use it at all. He said he had enjoyed it very much. He also said that he hoped I would become a Boy Scout as soon as I was old enough to join.

It was just the beginning of our friendship, which did not end until his death. I have been fortunate to have had many long-term friends during my very happy lifetime, and much of my happiness was because of them.

By the time I was three years old, I had learned that I enjoyed staying in hotels and traveling. Three years before I was born, my mother and dad had purchased a fifty-room summer hotel called the Bellevue Hotel in Beach Bluff, Massachusetts, part of the town of Swampscott. It was open from late April until the foliage ended in October. I just barely remember running along the wooded walkway or long porch, so popular with guests who enjoyed the rocking chairs.

The New Ocean House was a large and wonderful luxury hotel on the ocean a short distance away. Mother and Dad became fast friends with the owner, and when the New Ocean House was full, they would send their guests to the Bellevue.

(Just a quick thought: The son of the owner of the New Ocean House was killed in World War II. His father never recovered from his loss, and the hotel suffered and finally closed. It was a very sad turn of events.)

I loved all the guests. Many came back each year. Mother was an excellent hotel manager and was also an excellent cook, and her hired cooks knew they had to be very successful if they wanted to keep their jobs. She was always checking their attitudes and skills.

Mrs. Helen Dickenson spent her summer with Mother and Dad the very first year the hotel was open in 1924. She'd come for a week but stayed the whole summer. She returned in 1925 and in 1926. I was born just after the summer hotel rush, and Mrs. Dickenson was still there. From that day on, we had the pleasure of a permanent friend. She always called my mother "Pitter Patter" because mother never slowed down during work hours. As Helen aged, she lived in Boston in a fine hotel year-round. She remained with us until the family hotel was sold. Mother and I visited her in Boston at least once a year until her death. Her last Christmas card to us mentioned the Christmas card that I had sent to her in 1945 from South Korea, while I was in the navy. Friendship is a great gift from our Creator, and it deserves an important place in our lives.

Mother's chef made a different type of muffin each day. One day she noticed many had not been touched. She went to Mrs. Dickenson and asked her if she knew what was wrong.

Mrs. Dickenson said, "The guests didn't want to complain or embarrass you, but the muffins have little white worms in them." Mother was really upset. She looked at the muffins and found that the "little white worms" were actually shredded coconut. (Shredded coconut was just then sold for the first time.)

One night, a couple of her guests did not show up for dinner. Mother asked about them and found out that the husband was very ill. The man's wife was very religious and did not believe in doctors, and after the first night, the husband died. Mother took the mattress, sheets, towels, blankets, and pillows from the couple's room and burned them so that the returning guests would know that they were not using anything that had been involved in that sick man's death. Many of her guests remained friends for years.

The Bellevue Hotel was a fun place for a little boy. I made myself known to all. I tried very hard to build a real reputation of striving for attention. I have been told I was successful. Starting at the age of three, I learned about what adults called "panhandling." I would walk from guest to guest as they sat relaxing in their rocking chairs, and their candy and cookie offerings came easily and often.

Mother managed the hotel and the dining room for several years. Then I came along. My dad had been offered an important job as the purchasing agent for the Commonwealth of Massachusetts for all meat and perishables that provided three meals a day, 365 days a year, for the forty-four thousand people in the state hospitals and prisons. Here was more proof of Mr. Snyder's true friendship. He told my dad how much he would be missed when he accepted his new job. He also told Dad to take the offer because it had the security of being a civil service position. Even then, Mr. Snyder was expecting serious financial trouble for the whole country, and he was right. The Great Depression was close at hand.

Mother and Dad decided to sell the Bellevue Hotel to their chef, Anton, and his wife, Leila Squilari. I remember them so well. They were a very nice couple, and we all remained friends. Just before the sale was completed, Mother began seeking a family home for us.

The Squilaris kept the hotel for a number of years, long enough that I was able to go back to the hotel as a grown boy and see what they had done with it. They were delightful people and worked very hard to make a go of the hotel but finally had to sell it. They moved to Tennessee, where they were able to get another inn and continued to make a living. We used to send my school trousers to Anton, who would use them for work pants.

In the winter, when the summer hotel was closed, we rented an apartment from a very nice Italian family at 110 Lake Street in Arlington, Massachusetts. The family made their own wine, crushing the grapes with their feet to release the juice. When I was three, my mother was shocked when she saw them wash my feet and then they let me walk on their huge pile of red grapes in a very large metal container to help crush the grapes. All through my life, I have enjoyed being with the excitable Italians.

When it snowed, Dad would bundle me up, put me in a box on a sled (to keep me from falling off), and take me out on Spy Pond, close to where we were living. We would run and slide for an hour at a time. At this point, Dad was fifty-one years old and very happy to have a son. Still, it must have been difficult for him to change his entire outlook on life. It was the start of my wonderful relationship with my dad, which continued for thirty loving years, until he died in 1956 at the age of eighty-one. All of my memories of him give me joy. In my life, it's difficult for me to think of a greater loss than that.

INTRODUCING DAISY

10

My mother, Daisy Chase, at the age of twelve, was invited to live with her oldest sister, Alice, who was twenty-two and married to Howard Lindsay. They lived on a farm that overlooked the beautiful Lake Memphremagog, a lake that is very dear to our whole family. At that point, the lake was three miles wide and about twenty-eight miles long. About 80 percent of the lake is in Quebec, Canada. Alice and her family lived close to that lake—and some still do—for over one hundred years. Alice was still in the family home on the lake when she died in 1966 at the age of eighty-six.

Daisy was invited to live with Alice and Howard so that she could attend high school in Newport, Vermont, as there was no high school in Lyme, New Hampshire, where she was living. The school was about three and a half miles down the railroad track in a straight line. If there was a car going in that direction, she had a ride to school. If there was no ride available, she rose very early in the morning and walked the three and a half miles, usually alone, on the railroad track. She memorized the train schedules, which were made up of trains between Newport and Sherbrook, Quebec. She could not ride on them, and she had to be careful they did not ride on her.

(As an aside, in about 1941, a judge from Portland, Oregon, arrived for a stay at the Red Cottage, a bed and breakfast later known as the Lindsay Lodge, bringing with him his wife and grown daughter. My memory is that they came at least twice. They loved it and were willing to drive six thousand miles to visit Aunt Alice and all. At breakfast one morning, Aunt Alice came dressed in a very pretty zip-front bathrobe. The judge looked at her and said, "Mrs. Lindsay, may I zip your zipper to just an inch above your knee, and if I should zip further, would you think it ill of me?")

Mother's other sister, Mabel, had been living on her own for about two years. She was a freethinking and pretty young woman. Unfortunately, she was caught up in working where alcohol was available and some drugs as well. Even back then, the two problems were at work spoiling lives. When she was in her mid-twenties, she met a Native American, Luther "Bob" Blackbird. He was a very fine man. He was a hunter and trapper and guide in the Adirondack Mountains of New York State. Bob Blackbird fell in love with Mabel. They were married, and he took her to his home in the mountains. He was attentive, kind, and loving, and he gave her an entirely new life.

Mabel became a very good shot with a rifle. She helped him with all his chores that hunters and trappers must tend to daily. They were happy. Unfortunately she died when she was thirty-four. Bob remained a close friend of our family throughout his life and was particularly kind to me.

Walter, mother's brother, endured a very difficult time. He was only eight years old when he was sent to live with a farm family. The agreement was that he would live with the family and work for them. Farming is a never-ending work schedule. In a family farm, there are many times when there are not enough farmhands to complete all of the tasks. At age eight (or nine or ten or eleven), you are the lowest person in the work line, so you are faced with the worst jobs because you can't avoid them and because you like to eat. Walter worked very hard during his entire life. He married, raised a family of three girls and one son, and lived to be 105 years old. My mother, my dad, and I loved him.

Mother was very capable. She worked hard in high school. As she got older, she dated, but because she lived on the Lindsay farm, and there were very few automobiles, dating was not easy. Being with Alice was the bright spot in her life. Alice loved her, and she loved Alice. I have wondered if she could have grown to be the remarkable woman she became if there had been no Alice.

She finished high school and was offered an opportunity to live in Haddonfield, New Jersey, with the Melendy family, who were very educated and well placed, to help with their younger children. It was a wonderful experience for her at just the right time in her life. Daisy had been without her mother most of her life. Mrs. Melendy helped her to learn the fine points of keeping a home well organized, such as mending and dressmaking, cleanliness, and helping to care for children when ill. She also learned to be a very fine cook.

After she had been there for three years, the time came for her to leave the Melendy family and return to the Lowell, Massachusetts, area where some of her original family were living. She was a changed young woman. She knew that it was possible to build a good life with many benefits, and she was fortunate to have been with a family who made her one of its members while she was with them. They remained her friends as long as they lived. As her son, I received the benefits of her early education every day.

Once she was back in Lowell, she applied for work at a store named the Bon Marche. She was in sales work for the first time, and she loved it. Small bonus awards made her even more excited. One day she heard about the direct-mail advertising the store was using. She was excited when she learned that the store bought the advertising from an outside salesman.

She did her research and learned the company selling the service to the store was named Samson and Murdock, and it was in Boston. She took time off from Bon Marche and applied for a sales job with S&M when she was about twenty-five years old. The manager at S&M told her she was a woman; I am sure she was aware of that. His point was that there was no salary, just commission, and women did not do such things, suggesting she would fail. That did it. Now she had to prove she was better than most.

The manager gave in, sure that after a day or two, she would quit—but that was a word that was not in her vocabulary. She took the job. She had engraved business cards designed with her name, surrounded by the little flowers after whom she was named, white and yellow daisies.

She had learned about this kind of sales from the store where she had been working. So why not try other stores like it? What was the biggest store in Boston? It was Jordan Marsh and Company. Somehow, she got to Mr. Marsh's office. She was young, pretty, and aggressive, and she had her engraved business cards with daisies on them. Mr. Marsh had a secretary, who took her card in to show him (and, I suspect, make comments). As she was standing there, Mother heard a loud voice call out, *"Daisy! Get in here!"*

Mother said she had a wonderful interview. Mr. Marsh gave her a huge order. She took the order back to her manager at S&M, and he was stunned. He immediately tried to put her on salary, but the commission was so large that she got educated in an instant. The big money in sales is almost always commission only. When she met my dad for the first time, she learned that he too was on commission only. I think it made her know he was a strong person.

Later in my life, I met three different men who were in love with her but not right for her. She was single until she was thirty-one, when she married my dad, who was fourteen years older and a widower. She and my dad remained friends with those three men until each one took that last journey.

At the age of twenty-nine, Daisy was making a good living doing what would, at that time, normally be considered "man's work." She was working for Samson Murdock in Boston, selling direct-mail advertising to businesses.

She tried to sell her direct-mail advertising to a garage and auto man, Glenn Whitham. He introduced her to a friend of his, George Perkins, who was a top salesman for Batchelder & Snyder, a large and highly respected meat and perishables food supplier for hotels. George's territories were the Adirondacks in New York in the summer and Florida in the winter. Dad did such an outstanding job that he and the company's owner, Frederick Snyder, became lifelong friends. I grew to love Mr. Snyder, and I know Dad did too. In both Dad's life and my own, friends have been very important. As I look back over the years, I find many of my most joy-filled moments have been because of my friends.

World War I was a huge challenge. George was too old to serve and was deeply troubled because his wife, Grace, of nearly twenty years had died just a year ago. There were no children, and George was alone.

Daisy, at twenty-nine, was single and a powerful worker. Dad, who was in his forties and now a widower, was very attracted to her.

In 1920, George was forty-nine, and Daisy was thirty-one. They both had automobiles and were doing very well, but they were both lonely. George's wife was gone, and Daisy's brother and sister were in another state. They were walking down Boylston Street in Boston, holding hands, when a friend of George's pulled up beside them in his automobile. He said to George, "This is my brand-new car. I just picked it up. George, why don't you marry that girl? The two of you were made for each other. Marry Daisy, and I'll give you my new car for a weeklong honeymoon." What the friend didn't know was that George and Daisy were walking to her minister's home, where they planned to be married that afternoon.

Just think, once again, of how miracles work! George was fourteen years older than Daisy, but for them it was perfect. More proof that miracles really do work if you just make it easy for them.

DAISY'S ACCIDENT

11

This would be a good place to introduce myself. My name is George William Perkins, II. I was named for my father, and to make it easier for everyone, I was called Bill.

In 1926, George and Daisy Perkins were in love. He was fifty years old, and Daisy was thirty-six. They were a happy couple in their sixth year of married life. As mentioned, it was a second marriage for George, as Grace, his first wife, had died in 1917.

In April 1926, Daisy was in the back seat of a touring sedan driven by an elderly friend. The driver suffered a stroke, and his right foot was on the accelerator when his body became rigid. The car jumped forward and control was lost. The car went off the highway and rolled over. Daisy was badly injured. There were no seat belts back then.

She was taken out of the wrecked automobile and rushed to the nearest hospital. Lifesaving surgery was needed. Dr. Mixter saved her life. While in the hospital, she learned, much to her surprise and pleasure, that she was pregnant. It would be her first and only pregnancy. When she told George that he would soon be a father, he was stunned. George had been married to Grace Webster for nearly twenty years, and there were no children. He and Daisy had been married for six years.

We are all glad that my dad and I resembled each other. Many people enjoy playing with such situations. George could hardly believe it. Both he and Daisy were happy about the news, but George was stunned that he would soon be a father at the age of fifty-one.

Daisy was also concerned. By this time, she and George owned and managed the summer hotel, and George was chief purchasing agent of meat and perishable food for the hospitals and prisons in the Commonwealth of Massachusetts. Daisy was the manager of their hotel and in full charge of the dining room, as well as the other services required by the hotel guests. She managed a staff of over twenty people.

Daisy was concerned that the guests would be distracted if they knew that she was pregnant. It was now May, and the summer hotel was about to open. She was only four months into her nine-month schedule. She decided to keep her condition private as long as she could. She let her guests know that she was gaining weight and blamed it on her chef's excellent cooking.

Many of the hotel guests had been there before, becoming friends who returned every year. Daisy was well versed in the way food should be prepared and served. Her guests were happy and well fed. Near the end of the summer season, well into August, some of her friends realized that she would soon become a mother. Many were amazed that she had made it through the season and handled the many situations all hotels have in serving the public.

Finally, the long-awaited day arrived. Thirty-seven-year-old Daisy was taken to the hospital in Salem, Massachusetts, where her little boy was delivered by cesarean section. George rushed to the telephone to call his mother and tell her she had a grandchild.

His mother answered his call, and before he could speak, she said, "I am a grandmother, and I have a grandson."

George was stunned. How could she have known of the birth only thirty minutes earlier when she was in Nashua, New Hampshire? A nurse from Nashua was working in the hospital that day; knew George's mother and had called her. George did not get the chance to tell his mother that his first and only child—me—was born.

Dad could not believe he didn't have the opportunity to be the first to tell his mother about her only grandchild. I believe that bothered him deeply. I can easily understand his reasons. He was a very special man, and I was a very lucky child.

MISSED BOTH TREES

12

Mother (Daisy) was driving Glenn Whitham from Boston to Nashua, New Hampshire. It was a warm spring day, and all seemed well with the world. Mother was cruising along, as usual, at maximum legal speed. I suspect that Glenn was holding on to anything he could find that seemed to be solid. When a truck cut in front of them, a crash was inevitable.

Mother, who was about thirty years old, spun the steering wheel to the right, missed the truck by inches, and—still at high speed—headed for two large trees growing about five feet apart. She drove her automobile between the two trees, missing both by a paper-thin measurement, and stopped the car between them. It was so tight that neither door in the two-door car could be opened. She sat still in her seat for a moment while Glenn, gasping for air, said in a rather loud voice, "You got yourself in here; now get yourself out." Mother told me that Glenn was as white as a sheet and was perspiring profusely.

I remember being with my dear mother on the salt flats beside Great Salt Lake in Utah in 1946 when she was close to sixty years old. I watched her floor the accelerator in our big Oldsmobile and hit over one hundred miles per hour where the world record had been set on the Salt Flats.

By the time she was over eighty years old, none of my family wanted to drive with her. I can understand their feelings, but I don't remember her having an accident of any consequence. She was unique in many ways.

MOTHER'S LETTER TO HER SISTER

13

TODAY, THE REASON I see life in the way I do became apparent to me. My research turned up a page of musings written by my mother on July 8, 1942, at the age of fifty-three. I was sixteen. Her written words are difficult to read because the ink has faded, but I've copied them here:

July 8, 1942

As I write a card to send to my sister on her 63rd birthday, I realize I too am older growing, Life, how we love it all. Life when a baby, Life when childhood is innocent, Life as it grows into young womanhood or manhood, Life with its careless worries while we are matured. Life of our 2nd childhood, I Love it all. Life! Life! How I love to live in this marvelous, mysterious, beautiful world. Such glorious living in things all about us. Trees and flowers for beauty, brooks and rivers for activity. Stones and mountains for solidness and thinking. Color of our rainbow - everywhere. Thrills and sentiment. War! Dastardly thing. Life we live it even through War with anticipation of a glorious victorious ending even the battlefields, the conquerors those whom fall or those whom survive. Each one feels that thrill of Life, the sentiment of our Great God our King.

—Daisy A. Chase Perkins

When God takes one of our loved ones, words do not seem to mean all that we want them to mean. It's the feel of the heartbeat, the press of the hand. The very nearness that seems to put the depth of our souls into our words, at a time like this prayer, seems to draw us all closer. At eventide, just remember we will be praying that God bless you and keep you and give you divine strength, understanding, and all that is good.

This was the source of all of my twenty-five years at home. My dad backed up his wife and my mother completely and gave his total love to both of us. Today, when I found this writing by my mother and was able to decipher it, I felt as if I knew the answers to many of my questions of why I am like I am.

SEEING MOTHER CRY

14

On December 10, 1936, I saw my mother cry. She was a very strong woman, but she believed that tears had a kind of cleansing ability when you were deeply touched by some special happening. I was just ten years old, and it was quite late in the evening. Dad and Mother were in bed, and I must have been lonely because I remember getting in bed with them just as my dad turned on his radio. (This was before television.) Both of my folks seemed to be waiting for something to happen.

Suddenly, an announcer on the radio asked for a moment of silence while the station opened up contact with a radio station in London, England. I noticed that Mother was holding Dad's hand. She did that a lot, but this time it seemed different somehow.

A voice with a British accent spoke in a very quiet sort of way and said that in a moment or two, we would be connected to the King of England, who was planning to make a very serious personal announcement that was being broadcast to the entire world.

King Edward VIII spoke in a very serious and careful way. He said, "At long last I am able to say a few words of my own." This would end up being an evening of many words between my dad and my mother. Dad had tears in his eyes, a little like my mother. This had to be a very serious situation. Dad never cried.

Looking back to that night so long ago and now being older, with a wife and sons of my own, I understand what a highly personal and private speech we were listening to, unlike any other that I have heard.

It was the voice of a man who was the king of a great country with many millions of people over whom he ruled. He was the emperor of another large country as well. He was telling the world that he was giving up all of his enormous power, position, wealth, and so much more to be able to marry the woman he loved beyond anything else that life held for him. I can understand the tears in the eyes of both my mother and my dad. In fact, I have a few of my own now as I type.

Even the age of ten is not too early in life to have serious memories that last as long as you do.

ALMOST DIED, IF NOT FOR MOTHER

15

Milton Britton was a senior in high school when I was a sophomore. He used to walk by my home almost every Saturday and Sunday, and after a while, we began to talk. One day he stopped and asked me if I had ever hiked around Swain's Pond, which was about a mile away. I had ridden around it with my dad, but we had never stopped. There was quite a lot of woodland around it and no activity.

Milt told me, "I've made a small camp in the woods. I love the privacy and the wildlife that lives there." Suddenly, he looked at me. "We're friends," he said. "Would you like to walk with me? I'll be walking back about suppertime."

I was delighted. The timing was perfect. Mother was shopping. I carefully called to Dad, who was involved with working on his automobile. "Milton asked me to walk with him. Can I go?"

"When will you be back?" Dad asked.

"Before supper."

Without a lot of thought, he said, "Sure, but be careful." He knew Milton was a friend of mine and older.

It was a beautiful day and an easy walk. When we arrived at the pond, Milt led the way into the woods on a rough path. In a few minutes, we came into a little clearing, and he said, "We made it. This is my camp." He pointed to a huge pile of dead brush.

"Where?" I asked.

He walked over to the brush pile, leaned way over it, and picked up a section of the heavy brush that turned out to be his doorway. He had built a room about seven feet across and five feet high. He had made a framework covered with a waterproof canvas and then covered the whole thing with brush, even to his totally unseen entrance. Then he had carefully raised the floor so that when it rained, the water would not get inside. It was amazing.

There can't be a lazy bone in his body, I thought, *and he sure is a kind of loner.*

I knew I had been shown something special. Our friendship blossomed from there. That night we made it back by supper. Mom had quietly told off Dad because he wasn't quite sure what I had done or where I had done it, but my being back by supper saved him.

That night opened the door between Milton and my mother; she found him unusual. He never mentioned his father. In the next few months, Milt and I spent quite a lot of hours together. He was always working on something. He loved to work on old metal pieces. He had found a piece of iron about two feet long. As he studied it, he realized it was the back end of an old musket. All but two feet of the seven-foot weapon was missing, cut off.

The tiny hole that allowed the spark to enter the back end of the musket and ignite the black powder that would explode and drive the ball toward the target was closed with rust. It was so old and rusted that to most people it would have been no more than a short, heavy stake in a garden. But not Milton. He was thinking about the Fourth of July and how he could come up with a way to use firecrackers. He needed to clean out that tiny hole, so he took his drill, put the old pipe up on his workbench in his vice, and steadied the other end with his left hand. Holding the drill in his right hand, he pressed the drill against the little hole with his chest and began the drilling.

He must have caused a spark because—beyond imagination—there was still dry black powder inside that rusted musket, and it exploded. The inside of his left hand was badly burned and damaged. He was in great pain; he was alone at that moment and needed help. Our friendship had become special. He called my mother, and, like always, Daisy reacted instantly.

She rushed to her car, and in less than ten minutes, she was at Milton's home, wrapping his badly damaged hand and then driving him to the hospital. She stayed with him through the doctor's treatment and contacting his mother. She drove him home and made him as comfortable as she could. She contacted a doctor who lived across the street from Milton's home and made an appointment for the next day. Then she came home to feed Dad and me dinner, with her story for dessert. One month later, she was told she had prevented the loss of his entire left hand.

At his little woodland camp, I shared lunch with him one day, only to learn, after eating, it was a cooked gray squirrel. There wasn't much meat.

Milton and I stayed in touch for many years.

CHANGUINOLA

16

My dad's first wife, Grace, was to remain in Nashua for the year he was away in Panama. He would have room, board, and transportation, so most of his salary was banked. During his first year there, Dad lived with two friends. If a stranger arrived, they would invite him to lunch. They kept a twelve-foot boa constrictor on a screened-in porch. They had great fun putting their guest on the porch to wait for lunch. Quite often, the guest would suddenly see that large snake move and would leave in such a rush that it would be right through the screen door without opening it!

After a year he brought Grace and his brother Harry and his wife, Delia, down to join him. He also brought down his mother, father, and their dog. They stayed for two years.

Each year when Dad came home for his vacation leave, he would go to Atlantic Avenue in Boston and visit the used-clothing stores. He would buy used hats that were out of fashion and would take a trunk load back to Panama. The native people absolutely loved those hats! He always made a handsome profit by selling them.

Sharks were very active in the waters near Bocas del Toro in Panama. Dad and his friends would save food scraps and feed the sharks, especially at night, while standing on one of the railroad bridges. They also liked to take a sidecar down the tracks, hunting for various animals with a searchlight.

In 1982, my wife, Mildred, and I took her dad and our son Clifton to Costa Rica. We attended a convention in San Jose and then rented a car and drove to Panama; we wanted to see where Dad had lived and worked. At the border of Costa Rica and Panama was a bridge. It was against the law to take a rented automobile out of Costa Rica. For about two hours, we "discussed" going over that bridge with the constabulary of Costa Rica. Finally, with a considerable "gift" to the guards, we were permitted to drive across the bridge. We had to notify the Panamanian army that we were going to cross.

It was nearly midnight. A colonel met us, took over driving, and stayed with us until we reached Changuinola Junction, a really small town with only one hotel. The hotel gave us a sheet and a pillow. Our room had no windows and was truly an inside room. Mildred had never seen a place like it, and she refused to undress. Instead, she put the sheet on a very bad mattress and lay down on the bed in her slip, hugging her handbag. The bed collapsed in the center, and she ended up in sort of a V position. There was no bath, and it was very hot in the windowless room.

She was remarkable! She took it with a sweet, questioning smile, wondering—I am sure—why she'd ever married me. Dad and Clifton had a room with windows, but it was very tropical and very hot.

The next morning we took the narrow-gauge railroad to Bocas del Toro. I discovered that the frame and wheels of the train that had been Dad's were still in use after seventy years. The body of the railroad cars had been rebuilt out of quarter-inch steel plates. The train was filled with little children going to school.

We talked about Dad, Grace, and his folks going down and staying in Panama in 1910, where they lived in a cottage in the jungle. As I've mentioned, it was on a huge banana plantation owned by the United Fruit Corp, and they put a sign over the door that read NASHUA.

The first banana was brought to the United States by ship from Jamaica by Captain Jesse H. Freeman for the United Fruit Company, based in Boston. George W. Perkins Sr. helped raise bananas in Costa Rica and Panama from 1908 to 1912 for the same company. Both of these men were related by marriage without knowing it.

Postcard of United Fruit Company

Banana Harvest, Costa Rica
Antiwarsongs.org

It was such a thrill for me to walk where Dad had worked so hard and for so long. Driving along the Panama Canal, I imagined what it must have been like, building it almost by hand. Dad had been with Teddy Roosevelt and his headstrong daughter on the train that took them through the canal before the water was allowed in.

A story that my dad told about being in Panama is worth repeating. A sideline track of the Changuinola Railroad ran into the jungle and ended at a banana plantation. Dad was in charge of the train. A huge pile of bananas needed to be picked up. The native people who lived and worked on the plantation were to load the train.

There was a small shack next to the pile of bananas, built on stakes to stay dry in wet weather. Long ago, two men fighting with machetes over a woman killed each other in that shack. It was late in the afternoon and getting dark, and the natives were very superstitious. The darker it got, the more nervous the natives became.

My dad had a funny sense of humor at times. He left the train, went into the brush in back of the shack, and crawled under it. When the last bunch of bananas had been loaded, it was quite dark, and Dad began to groan. He used to say all speed records were broken by the fleeing natives, who thought they were hearing angry spirits of the dead men! My dad never seemed to be afraid of anything or anyone, even though snakes, spiders, rats, fire ants, and who knows what lived under those old houses up on stakes.

The canal caused the loss of the lives of thousands of men. Yellow fever decimated the French. US Army engineers had to battle the mosquitoes, and malaria also took a heavy toll. My dad suffered his last malaria attack when he was in his late seventies.

In spite of everything, the end result made the canal one of the seven man-made wonders of the world. I have loved having pictures in my office that Dad brought back when he finally came home to Nashua.

When I was a sophomore in high school, Dad was hit very hard with pneumonia and a final attack of malaria left over from working in Panama. He ran a temperature of 105 for three days! We packed him in ice to cool him off and bring down his temperature. At the onset, he weighed 230 pounds. In three days, he lost forty pounds and should have died. He sweated so heavily that the sheets were drenched. We changed the sheets every hour, twenty-four hours a day, for three days. How that man survived that terrible attack is beyond our comprehension, but he did survive, although he was left with diabetes.

Six months later, we thought he was having a heart attack and rushed him to the Deaconess Hospital in Boston. It turned out that he was having a diabetic attack that was putting him into a diabetic coma. I was about twenty-two at the time. The Joslin Clinic was the best diabetic clinic in the world at that time. Dad was in a four-bed intensive care unit for eight weeks. All four of the men, including dad, were very ill due to diabetic comas. Only my tough, hardworking dad survived. With today's advanced knowledge and medication, I believe the others could have survived too. Dad lived to the age of eighty-one but never regained his full weight. He was about 160 pounds when he died. The Joslin Clinic gave my father an award that said he had lived fifteen years longer than expected.

UNLICENSED DENTIST

17

Bob Longley went to Panama and Costa Rica with Dad about 1910. He had to decide how to make a living and survive. Dad and Bob became very close friends, a friendship that would last for the rest of their lives. Bob had an idea. He purchased a set of dental "pliers" and became a traveling dentist of sorts. If one of the natives had a painfully aching tooth, Bob would remove it with the right-sized pliers. (He hoped he got the right tooth!) He charged twenty-five cents. Considering the pay scale for workers in that hot climate, that was a substantial fee. He pulled teeth without anesthesia or follow-up. How times do change.

When Bob returned home to Massachusetts, he found ways to improve his standard of living. He married Anne and bought a lovely home in Lynn, a half block from the ocean. They had four children, two boys and two girls. Bob Jr. and Miner were much older than me and fine men. I fail to remember the names of the girls, but I do remember visiting one of the girls when I was working in Los Angeles. She had married one of the best known pro big-league football players.

Bob installed an outdoor shower at his home. He was so close to the ocean, and his children often came home covered with sand from the beach. An outdoor shower just made practical sense. But to me, at age nine or ten, it seemed awesome. I didn't get to the beach that often. It just seemed like such a luxury because it had both hot and cold water outdoors.

The last time I was with Bob was when he visited Mother and me in our home in Melrose, Massachusetts. He wanted to say goodbye, although we did not realize it at the time. Dad had left us, and Bob truly cared about us. All of the Longleys called my mother "Chasie." Bob had known her before she and Dad were married, when her last name was Chase.

Bob smoked a pipe. It's now about seventy years after that last visit, and I still enjoy the memory of his visit. This kind, very special man sat in our living room, smoking his pipe, using the most fragrant tobacco I have ever experienced. It is a very warm memory. Thank you, Bob.

FINANCIAL WIZARDS

18

It's interesting to think of Mother and Dad's situation when they married in 1920. His first wife's health expenses, accrued before her death in 1917, left an outstanding debt that needs to be understood. In 2008, $12,000 was still a substantial debt that needed to be paid, but in 1920, a decent house could be purchased for less than $10,000. A new car could be purchased for $600, bread was about 12¢ a loaf, and milk cost about 5¢ a quart.

It took the earnings of both Mother and Dad for three years to pay off that medical cost. Then they bought the Bellevue Hotel for $30,000. It took them five years to pay off that debt. Mother really loved Dad, even though he was heavily in debt. He was traveling as a salesman much of the time. She knew she would have to continue working—this was at a time when most married women became housewives. Their marriage was strong and filled with love and cooperation. I can't remember a single serious problem between them, and I grew up surrounded by real love.

By the time they sold the hotel, their position had changed. When I was born in 1926, they had owned the hotel for three years. When they added the tasks of a new baby to Mother's function as hotel manager and Dad's traveling, selling the hotel seemed logical. When it was sold in 1928, for the first time in her adult life, my mother could stop working and put all her time into being a wife and mother. She was just turning forty.

They were advised to invest their savings in the Gas and Electric Company as a sure thing. What no one was thinking about was the Great Depression, which began in 1929 and ran to 1939. When people could not pay their gas or electric bills, the company failed. It was an expensive lesson.

Cooperative banks were suddenly popular. You could open your own account and put as little as a dollar in it or more if you wished. The bank paid interest on your deposits, and that interest accumulated. My mother really liked this. It was a safe way to invest. She used her savings accounts in this manner for the rest of her life and was still putting a dollar away until the last three months of her life at age ninety-five.

FRENCH HILL, NASHUA, NEW HAMPSHIRE

19

My dad's mother's maiden name was Paige. Mark Paige, her father, was a homebuilder in Nashua, New Hampshire. He built the homes on Paige Avenue, which was named for him, located at the top of French Hill. The last home on the left side of Paige Avenue, number 14, was built by Mark Paige for his daughter, Ella Paige Perkins, and her husband, William Nathaniel Perkins. It is now a two-family home; I am trying to find out the year it was completed.

There was a good view of the farmland that stretched from the bottom of French Hill all the way to the Merrimack River. At that time, the river had no flood control dam north, to where it had its beginning. In 1936, the water began to rise very quickly. A farmer who raised big red English hogs on the flat farmland near the river was away. The river rose, and the water allowed the hogs to float over the fence that contained them.

His six-hundred-pound boar, with his large tusks and red color, was a rare animal. I have been told that pigs have trouble swimming because of their short front legs, but that hog floated and swam all the way to Newburyport, Massachusetts, a distance of at least forty miles, where it made headlines when it came out of the river. What kind of a strange red animal with huge tusks had been seen in the Merrimack River? What could it be? Where did it come from? Now we know.

My dad was born in Pelham, New Hampshire, in 1875. That means that William and Ella were living there at the time. They had just two sons. Harry was my dad's younger brother.

Harry and his wife, Delia, never had any children. My mother told me that Harry was Protestant and Delia was Catholic, and neither would agree to bring up a child in the other's religion. If that is true, it's very sad. They would have made good parents. All of my memories of them are happy ones. While I was young, our two families were together a great deal.

When my grandmother died in 1942, her very nice antique card table was left to Aunt Delia. While I was growing up and visited her and Uncle Harry, we played games on that card table. When Aunt Delia died, following Uncle Harry's death, she left that table to me in her will. It now sits (and is often used) in our living room. I enjoy that fine, old, well-used family gift, which was left to me very unexpectedly. It carries forward other happy memories of how pretty she was, her enjoyment of lavender soap in her bathroom, and her pleasant fragrance as soon as she opened her door.

20

In 1916, Dad joined the Batchelder and Snyder Hotel Food Supply Company, which specialized in handling meat and perishables. He already was Mr. Snyder's top salesman. His territory was New York in the summer and Florida in the winter, with overlapping times. Dad's work ethic was important to him. He gave his employer total attention and perfect expense reporting—always!

Dad's sales territory was New York's Adirondack Mountains in the summer. In 1919, a late-season blizzard hit when Dad was still on the road. It was so severe that Dad had to stop. The only place he could find was a small dance hall and inn, and because of the storm, there were no rooms available. The manager knew Dad and told him he could share a bed with the small band's drummer. Dad had been working and then fighting the blizzard for hours and was exhausted, so he accepted the offer. He went upstairs, found the room and the bed, and promptly went to sleep. He awoke in the morning with a person on either side of him, sound asleep. He was shocked, however, to see that they were both women! The band was an all-women dance band!

In 1917 my dad was away on a business trip in New York State. When he arrived home, he found his wife, Grace, dead in their Boylston Street apartment in Boston. He later learned she had suffered from a ruptured appendix and then pneumonia had set in. Her had health grown more and more troublesome. She had breathing difficulties and was admitted to the hospital. She was given a shot of morphine, a standard treatment back then. At home, her breathing grew worse, and she gave herself additional morphine, but she still needed help. A doctor lived in the same building, so Grace called him. He came up to her apartment and gave her morphine, not knowing she had just taken morphine. It killed her. Dad was left with about $12,000 in medical expenses. In today's currency, that would be more than $270,000.

About a year after Grace's death, Dad met Daisy Almira Chase. They were drawn to each other. Because she was selling direct-mail advertising for a major company, Dad introduced her to Frederick Snyder, his employer. They became immediate friends.

The Snyders invited George and Daisy to visit them at their home. Daisy and Mrs. Snyder enjoyed each other. That, too, was an inspiration for my dad. The difference in their ages was a concern to him, but it didn't seem to bother Daisy at all. She was in love. Dad proposed, and Daisy accepted.

It was shortly after that when, as you might remember, they were walking along Boylston Street, holding hands, when Dad's friend drove up next to them and offered his car for a weeklong honeymoon if Dad would marry Daisy.

Dr. Conrad of the Park Street Church in Boston married Mother and Dad on April 20, 1920. They drove up into the scenic White Mountains of New Hampshire on their honeymoon. In Whitefield, they had car trouble and had to stay overnight at a small inn. Dad signed in as man and wife, Mr. and Mrs. George Perkins. When Mother signed the registration page, she unthinkingly wrote "Daisy A. Chase" from habit. The innkeeper refused to let them have a single room with one bed. They had to rent two rooms and stay apart from each other because at ten o'clock at night, they had no way to prove they were married. Times do change.

BOY SCOUT POCKETKNIFE

21

My life has been guided by many people who helped me understand that life gives back to you what you ask of it, provided you pass along to others what you have been given by the people who have meant the most to you. I understand what I have just written. I doubt if anyone else understands it.

As I've mentioned, my dad was a top salesman for the Batchelder and Snyder Hotel Supply Company in Boston, and Frederick S. Snyder and my dad developed a close friendship that lasted until my dad's death. I've also mentioned that on my first birthday, Mr. Snyder sent me his own Boy Scout pocketknife, along with a note telling me, a one-year-old baby, that I should be a Boy Scout when I was old enough. I still have that knife.

Mr. Snyder was in charge of food supplies in the United States during the World War I years. He worked closely with President Herbert Hoover. In 1928, the president made a trip to South America on board the battleship *Maryland*. He wrote a letter of thanks to Mr. Snyder for information that Mr. Snyder had sent to him. The letter mentioned that the trip was successful. It was the first trip of its kind ever made by an American president and became a valuable part of our history.

Mr. Snyder wrote me a wonderful letter, explaining why the president had made this particular trip. It was so important that I have it framed on my office wall. When I was not much older than age two, those two letters became an important part of my education. What kind of a man would think to do such a thing for a baby of two? A very special man.

Eighteen years later, during World War II, I enlisted in the United States Navy. I was assigned to serve on the battleship *Maryland*. It was in dry dock in San Diego, having been repaired after being hit by two Japanese suicide bombers. I was privileged to be on her when she left to go back to the war in the Pacific. I felt that

I knew her well. After all, I had her name hanging on my wall at home, and I knew that she had carried the president on a very successful trip on December 6, 1928, when I was just two years old.

FREDERIC S. SNYDER
53 BLACKSTONE STREET
BOSTON, MASSACHUSETTS

3 January,1929.

My dear Bill:

It occurs to me that in view of our mutual enthusiasm for Mr. Hoover, the letter I am sending you herewith, written by Mr. Hoover, may be a nice thing for you to keep. It came to me this morning. It was written on board the battleship Maryland, on which Mr. Hoover made a trip from California to South America.

When you go across the street and play with a small boy or girl, you make a call on them. That is about what Mr. Hoover has been doing. His call was made on the chief officials of several nations in South America and was for the purpose of becoming acquainted with them and making them understand the friendly feeling which he and the people of the United States have for them. As President of the United States, he will undoubtedly have problems to solve connected with these nations. He can do this better after he has seen them and their people and become acquainted with their leading officials. This trip has been called a goodwill journey. You will notice in the last paragraph of the letter from President-elect Hoover that he says . . .We are having a pleasant journey; and so far the trip seems to be accomplishing the purpose for which we set out". No such journey as this was ever undertaken by any other president of the United States; therefore this letter will I think have some historical value and I am sending it to you with that idea in mind.

With very best wishes for a happy new year, which good wishes please share with your mother and father, I remain,

Yours very truly,

William Perkins, Esq.,
        110 Lake Street,
            Arlington, Massachusetts.

FSS - K.

Enclosure

HERBERT HOOVER

On Board,
U. S. S. Maryland,
December 6th, 1928.

Mr. Frederic S. Snyder,
53 Blackstone St.,
Boston, Mass.

My dear Mr. Snyder:

Many thanks for your kind
letter of November 21st which reached me today.

I have read Mr. Hammond's
address with a great deal of interest and
profit. I wish to thank you for sending it
to me.

We are having a pleasant
journey, and so far, the trip seems to be
accomplishing the purpose for which we set out.

Yours faithfully,

Herbert Hoover

HH:FK.

FREDERICK WAS THERE

22

Frederick Snyder was a very important man. During World War I, he worked for Herbert Hoover, who, quite simply, was in charge of the country's food. Frederick was also well-to-do, a millionaire when there were only a few of them. When Herbert Hoover ran for president of the United States, Frederick was there.

He wrote to President-Elect Hoover when he was on board the USS *Maryland*. He was the first president to make such a trip to countries in Central and South America to enhance relations. Mr. Hoover wrote to Mr. Snyder from aboard the ship. It was an important letter, and Mr. Snyder knew it would have great value in the future.

Even as early as 1921, Frederick Snyder was expecting major financial business problems. It took eight years for the Great Depression to hit. Even with the changes that all married couples experience, some good and others that would be nice to forget, the two families held on to their friendships.

When I was born in 1926, I was not aware of much of anything except being warm and well fed, but I already had a serious friend named Frederick S. Snyder. You'll remember he sent me his Boy Scout jackknife on my first birthday. His note that arrived with the knife included his saying he was very happy to give me his own Boy Scout jackknife and that I should use it very carefully. As I've mentioned, when I was two, I received the Snyder and Hoover letters from the battleship *Maryland*. Mr. Snyder wrote that the letter was important, and he sent me the original. (I have it now in our bank safe deposit box.) A copy of both letters is here for your interest.

In 1932 Frederick Snyder wrote to me from the Lincoln bedroom in the White House in Washington, DC. It was addressed to "Bill Perkins" and signed "Your partner, FS Snyder."

On January 3, 1929, when I was three, my parents received a letter addressed to "William Perkins, Esq." at our winter home, 110 Lake Street, Arlington, Massachusetts. I have it framed on the wall of my office in Nashua, and I value it most highly. This came from a very special man to a child. How wonderful kind, thoughtful adult friends can be to young children with, perhaps, far-reaching results in their life plans.

I received a gift every year until I was a grown man, and all of his gifts were his possessions before he sent them to me. They were all very personal. My first freshwater fly rod was custom-made for him out of bamboo by an expert. It was my twelfth gift. The note with it said that he loved that fly rod, and he hoped it would give me the great pleasure it had given him. He advised me to wear a life jacket if I was in a boat, but he said he preferred to fish for trout in small brooks and creeks.

The two families, his and mine, met at least once each year to "compare notes" all through my time in high school. Then came college and then an interruption for me to serve in the US Navy during World War II. My first ship assignment, ironically, was on board the old battleship *Maryland*, where I was a fire control specialist gunner. She had been hit by three Japanese kamikaze (suicide) planes and had been repaired. I went aboard her at the San Pedro Naval Base in Long Beach, California, in 1945. I felt like I knew that ship and could feel President Hoover writing to me.

When I was about twenty-three, Mr. Snyder took my mother and me out for lunch to a very fine restaurant. During dessert, Frederick told us about hunting squirrels. All the people in the restaurant learned he was there when he proceeded to demonstrate how he called squirrels when in the forest. Their attention did not bother him a bit.

On October 6, 1951, Frederick was a guest at Mildred's and my wedding. I have a photograph of the three men who have been the most important to me in my life: Mildred's father, Dr. Milton Boyle; my dad; and Frederick S. Snyder. It was a rather large wedding, with the reception held at the Baptist Church in Medford, Massachusetts. Then I learned that Mildred planned to go back to her family home to dress for our wedding trip. That meant, of course, more time could be spent with special guests and many of Mildred's very large family.

All of this needed to take place before we could leave for our first night together. It would be a night that I had waited for four years to win. If nothing got in the way, we would both be able to stop using the word *virgin*, except when referring to other anxiously waiting couples. As we went out of the front door and down the long front steps to our waiting car, Mr. Snyder put a small envelope in my hand and said, "Don't lose it!" It made our trip even more special, coming from him. When we opened it, there was a hundred-dollar bill! At that time, a hundred dollars was a large gift.

All through my life, I have watched wonderful men and women go out of their way to do unexpected, kind, friendly, caring things for others. I hope I have succeeded in passing on the same thinking and actions too.

THE MORE I TRAVEL

23

MY DAD REALLY believed that travel can be an ardent educator. He was correct. As I look back at all of my educational experiences, extensive travel takes first place for exciting learning. Here's a word or two that creeps in to explain what could be its downside:

> The more I travel, the more I know.
> The more I know, the more I can forget.
> The more I can forget, the more I forget.
> The more I forget, the less I know.
> So why travel?

When my dad finished his four years working in Panama and Costa Rica, he joined the Raymond Whitcomb Travel Organization as a tour conductor. This also tied him to another Boston company that carried groups of people in what they lovingly called the Great White Fleet. The groups for which he was responsible enjoyed his sense of humor, his total dedication to their pleasure, and his outstanding concept of how to sightsee.

When Dad decided that he would expand my travel education, he made sure that I knew about his experience with travelers who were not willing to sightsee but were still part of his group. Some of the people preferred to stay behind and read a book after they had already paid to sightsee. That simply drove my dear dad nuts. At the Grand Canyon, two people in his group who would not even get off the train.

He made certain that I traveled with my eyes wide open and was constantly inquisitive about everything. I knew that I had no choice, and—fortunately for me—I am naturally interested in just about everything.

DEATH VALLEY SCOTTY

24

In 1939, Dad decided to drive from Boston to Los Angeles and back using two different routes, which would allow us to visit the largest number of individual states. Dad had worked for four years in Panama during the construction of the Panama Canal, from 1908 to 1912. He knew that the general who was in charge of the canal project was also involved in the giant Boulder Dam project. The dam was completed in two-thirds of its allotted contract time and was dedicated and then completed by 1936. Seeing this highest dam in the world was a must on Dad's travel list. In order to reach this engineering wonder, our trip took us through a dusty, old, small western town on the road from Los Angeles to the dam. I was thirteen years old, and I was in Las Vegas, Nevada. Ten minutes later, I was out of Las Vegas, never even knowing it existed. I did not see all of the forty-eight states on that first trip.

Two years later, in 1941, Dad again drove on two different routes across our country. We drove through all of the remaining forty-eight states and completed his plan. Our travels took us, once again, through the faintly blossoming town of Las Vegas. The only memory I have of that small town is seeing a tiny hotel that was owned by a band leader whose name I recognized but cannot recall these seventy-three years later.

During World War II, my ship was being restored in the naval shipyard at San Pedro, which was close to Los Angeles. I hitchhiked to Vegas to see friends and family who were managing a motel on Lake Mead, near Boulder Dam. On my way, I passed through Barstow, California, a few hours outside of Vegas. This brings back a memory of my adopted grandfather.

Death Valley is close to Barstow. Death Valley Scotty was a well-known resident in the Valley and was a friend of Granddad's. Both of them had been working cowhands or prospectors, and Scotty was a true character. This was back about 1900.

Scotty had a thousand-dollar bill that he carried with him everywhere. In the Death Valley area, no one could make change for a thousand-dollar bill. Scotty knew it, so he would buy an item, knowing the shop owner could not make change, so it was "on the cuff." Scotty owed everyone for things he ostensibly tried to pay for, but no one could make change.

My adopted grandfather was very upset when he was stuck with paying for many of Scotty's purchases. He made a trip outside of the Valley, withdrew money, and carried it with him for two years. Scotty asked Granddad if he would drive him to Barstow to buy a new pair of boots. Scotty tried to pay with his thousand-dollar bill, and of course the clerk could not change it. Then a voice from the back of the store said, "Hold on there. I can change that bill."

Grandfather had carried the huge roll of one-dollar bills just for that moment. He counted out one thousand one-dollar bills, handed them to Scotty, and took the thousand-dollar bill. Scotty had to pay for his boots *and* carry that huge wad of ones. It was a good day for my grandfather.

He and Scotty were good friends until Scotty died. I have always been happy that I knew the old con man who could tell stories in his own special way. I offered him a cold glass of water once when it was over 110 degrees. He looked at me as he took the glass and said, "Here's to you, and here's toward you. If I hadn't seen you, I wouldn't have knowed you." Then he said, "Oh! It's water. Well, between the teeth and over the gums. Look out, stomach; here it comes," and he drank the entire glass. Scotty and his dog are both buried on a high spot near his castle where he lived. I have said hello and goodbye several times at his gravesite.

A very personal note about Scotty: My meeting Scotty when I was thirteen introduced me to a unique type of man. It made very little impression on me. I kind of liked him, but at thirteen, he was not in my world. We were invited to tour his castle, and that was exciting. The swimming pool was not yet finished and stood empty. I was fifteen when I learned more about Scotty. Dick Randall gave me valuable stories and a wonderful picture of Scotty, my grandfather, and Albert Johnson, Scotty's partner.

Death Valley Scotty   Dick Randall   Albert M. Johnson

Las Vegas has been in and out of my life for over seventy-five years. There have been many highs and a few lows in Vegas, as times have changed, and the town has become the only city of its kind in the entire world. Some years ago, I had an assignment that required me to study the Bellagio Hotel and its dancing waters. I had visited dancing waters in Singapore, but the waters at the Bellagio not only danced; they exploded. What a marvel they are when set to music by people with immense talent.

I enjoyed three days and three nights in the Wynn Resort. I spent over ten hours on photographic efforts to help me retain as much as possible in my memory after leaving. My wife and I continued our honeymoon, which has lasted for nearly sixty-three years, in one of Wynn's lovely bedrooms. We enjoyed a spacious bathroom, well equipped and maintained by a friendly housekeeper.

A simple light bulb burned out, so I called housekeeping, and I made a note of my call. There was a knock on my door in exactly eleven minutes. The bulb was replaced, and the room was inspected. The bulb was in a fixture at least nine feet over the desk. It was changed with a tool carried for just this purpose by a man who told us how important we were as guests of Wynn. He mentioned how happy he was to be working for Wynn.

FER-DE-LANCE

25

During his first year with the United Fruit Company, Dad needed to wear a pistol during working hours. Costa Rica is home to one of the most venomous snakes in the world. The fer-de-lance is an expert at hiding on the ground, surrounded by ground cover, and is very hard to see because of its color and markings. One place that particular snake seems to enjoy is a large banana plantation, just like the one my dad was working on. Dad needed to walk through a section of the plantation that was new to him, and suddenly, for no reason, he stopped and stood very still.

When he told me about his situation, I was fourteen. He was trying to explain something to me. I don't remember what it was, but I looked at Dad, and he looked different than I had ever seen him. He said, "Stay right here; I need to show you something." Dad was really different at that moment. He came back with a little leather box. I still have it. He took out a small, curved piece of jewelry. It was white and about two inches long. It looked like a bit of bone, larger on one end than on the other end. A gold cap on the larger end had a little gold chain attached, and I asked Dad if it could be worn on his necktie. He smiled and said, "Exactly right."

The gold cover on the smaller end was about a half inch long and was pointed. It was odd, even strange. He said, "Son, this is the tooth of a large fer-de-lance snake that nearly killed me. I came barely within his striking distance, but something made me stop and not move. I have no reason for why I actually froze. I didn't see a thing. The only thing I moved was my head and eyes. There, directly in my path, was the largest fer-de-lance I had ever seen. Without moving my feet at all, I was able to take my pistol and shoot the snake. I had just the smallest chance of living. The snake is famous for the amount of venom it produces, and that snake was two feet longer than any other I had seen.

"I removed one of the snake's poison-filled fangs; they all have two. Then I boiled the fang for two hours. When I came back to Boston, I had it made into a tie decoration, and this is it. Every time I think about it, I have to see it. It was the closest I have been to dying. If I had died, you, dear son of mine, would not be here. Just think about it."

SNAKE PROBLEMS

26

Dad was a special type of man. He did not enjoy drinking anything with alcohol in it. He never smoked, and saw no good return from gambling, so he passed it by. He was in love with his wife, Grace, and he had no interest in the native women. His sense of humor was wonderful, and as I've mentioned, you could hear him laugh from a distance. His work ethic was his pride and joy.

Dad talked a lot about his narrow-gauge railroad's problems with the large nonvenomous boa constrictor that enjoyed lying across the train tracks after they had swallowed some small animal, like a pig. A snake would grab the animal with its teeth and then wind its body around the animal, and each time the animal took a breath and exhaled it would tighten its coils and suffocate it. After eating, the snake often became lethargic with that large lump in its stomach, and if it was on the track, it could be large enough to derail a train. Dad would have to move the snake out of the train's way.

One of the boas was very large, about eighteen feet long. It was very heavy, having just enjoyed lunch. Dad could not make it move and finally had to kill it. He had the snake skinned and the skin cured, and when he came home for good, he brought the skin to Nashua. The skin was cured with arsenic and other chemicals. I still have that skin.

When I was in high school we left our German Shepherd, Zonta, in the basement for a few hours. When we arrived home, we found her in convulsions. She had found the rolled-up boa skin and had nibbled the edge of it. After forty years, the arsenic in that skin was still powerful. We rushed the dog to the veterinarian, and he saved her.

Zonta was a wonderful dog. When we bought Zonta, Dad had a hog farm in Wilmington, Massachusetts. His hired hand retired, and Dad was then seventy-one, so the farm was sold. Zonta had a litter of puppies. We gave away or sold all but one, a black shepherd named Monk that was very friendly. It had one ear that stood up straight, and the other one flopped over. The dog grew to be very big, weighing 120 pounds. Suddenly, the Cushman baker who delivered bread, the Hood milkman, and the mailman all stopped delivering. They were afraid of our dog! He would sit on the top step of our back porch, where all deliveries were made, and watch for the deliverymen. Even though he was very friendly, his overall appearance was menacing to these men.

We knew a farmer in Acton, Massachusetts, who raised chickens commercially. He was losing chickens to a family of red foxes. Monk was fully grown and needed more land to run on, so we gave him to the farmer. From the first day on the farm, not a single chicken was stolen by a single member of that fox family ever again.

We had given our German shepherd Zonta to another farmer friend, as she also needed more space to run. We were having supper and listening to the radio about six months later when we heard on the news that our dog named Zonta had just won a lifesaving medal from the Animal Rescue League. A horse was sinking in quick mud in a marsh on the farm where Zonta was living. She saw the horse and ran to the farmer, barking, and dragged the farmer to where he could see the horse. He got a rope and his truck, but by the time he reached the horse, only its head could be seen. He roped the horse and slowly pulled it out of the mud with his truck. We were very glad we had given our dog to that horse lover.

GRACE AGREED TO STAY HOME

27

As I write this, it is Father's Day 2017. It's a very special day for me. My three sons are a source of constant and loving contact. Without the greatest joy in my life, my sons' mother, Mildred, this could not have taken place. The most important single effort I have ever made and won was waiting out the four years it required to earn a yes from Mildred and our marriage on October 6, 1951.

This morning I find myself deeply involved with memories of that unique man who became my own dad on Friday, September 10, 1926, at two minutes past noon. At that moment, I lucked out. He too had won by marrying Daisy, my mother. But this is Dad's day, and he has most of my thoughts right now.

When Daisy wisely chose my dad for her first and only husband, it proved to be a remarkably good decision for my future. They had been married for six years when mother was nearly killed in an automobile accident. As I've mentioned, it was when she was in the hospital for lifesaving surgery that the doctor learned she was about three months pregnant. It proved to be her only pregnancy.

While Mother was overjoyed to learn she would become a mother at age thirty-seven, I have to wonder what occurred when she joyfully told my dad, age fifty-one, that he would soon become a father. After having been married to two women for close to twenty-six years, fatherhood was unexpected.

On this, my dad's day, I look at all I have been trying to compete with. Dad loved to work. He was very successful because he had a great voice, laugh, and attitude that attracted customers. He had one younger brother, Harry, who had a totally different approach to his life.

The Panama Canal was of real interest to Teddy Roosevelt. It was his consuming interest. He was counting the days and then the weeks and finally the years to its completion, with its awesome tasks and overall problems. The French had lost thousands of workers in its construction before giving up. Land was finally purchased from Colombia, and the country of Panama was created, with the United States owning the canal. In 1906, Dad had the opportunity to go to Panama to work on trains there. Grace agreed to stay at home, and Dad was offered a much higher income than he could have earned in Nashua. The canal was a very difficult engineering situation.

About 1907, the United Fruit Company offered Dad an opportunity to work their trains in their banana plantations in Panama and Costa Rica. The company's headquarters were in Boston. This meant that Dad could travel between Boston and the Central American countries on the Great White Fleet owned by the company.

Due to the health of Dad's wife, Grace, he never had anything to do with children. After his first working position at the age of thirteen, nearly all of his time was spent working with adults. He became a dad for the first time after several years of being in charge of many workers in Costa Rica and Panama with little education. They had totally different ways of living, with and without wives, and with borderline conditions that demanded very high degrees of control. This gave my dad the ability to cuss for close to half an hour without repeating himself.

I must make it totally clear that my dad never—not once—used a single swear word at me. Not even once! Of course, I was nearly perfect. That helped him a little. I do remember just once, when I was being a little impossible, hearing him say to my mother, "Daisy, you must take care of that boy because if I touch him, I just might injure him!"

Looking back on my childhood, I was with my dad, feeding hogs and caring for litters of little pigs on his hog farm. He bought the farm because he knew World War II was sure to blow up, and meat would become very scarce. Meat was a large part of his business. Dad had been appointed chief purchasing agent for meat and perishables for the Commonwealth of Massachusetts, used to feed the people in state hospitals and prisons.

Most weekends, we were working on his farm. It was about 1934 when he bought the acreage at the suggestion of Frederick Snyder, who had the experience of helping to feed the people of the United States during World War I. I do not remember Mr. Snyder ever being wrong when it came to food.

Dad would pack a lunch and include enough for me, and he would let me bring a friend. We would spend Saturday with the hogs and little pigs. I remember one young girl—she was about twelve or thirteen—from Melrose who was quite deaf. Dad liked her. She handled her hearing problem well. There were no good hearing aids. Her name was MacAnanny. She went out with us several times.

In my age group in Melrose, Massachusetts, there were very few families with working farms. Most of my school friends were into sports. At that time, my dad was almost ready to retire. He wanted me to become very good at raising carrier pigeons. I loved pigeons but not just any pigeons—carrier pigeons. He helped me build a coop for my pigeons on top of our two-car garage. We cut a hole in the back wall of the garage and built a screened area they could use, with a doorway that would only let them in.

Dad taught me to write messages and put them into tiny ankle bracelets on the carrier pigeons. We would put the pigeons into carrying cases and drive twenty miles away and then release them. We would drive back home and try to be there when they arrived at their nests. It was exciting in its own unique way.

My favorite was a beautiful maroon female I called Earphones. She had two white spots where earphones would go, and a band of white feathers connecting them. I really loved that pigeon. I would put a kernel of corn in my mouth, and she would hop on my shoulder and lean way over to eat all the corn right out of my mouth! My dear mother was convinced I was cause for concern.

Baseball, basketball, and football were not my thrill generators, much to the relief of my mother, who did not like contact sports. At sixteen, Dad made me start my training on how to shoot with rifles, shotguns, and handguns. In 1942 the population was small, and there were many old dirt roads with no one using them. Dad knew every one of them. Partridges are birds that can be delicious. They often settled down on the old dirt roads late in the afternoons to create dust that could fill their feathers and force the itching bugs out.

Dad would do the driving while I sat on the front hood of the sedan, over the engine, with my shotgun ready. Dad would drive slowly, and both of us would be partridge watchers. We were fortunate if we actually saw a few birds. We thought it was a great trip if we were close enough to have a clear shot at any bird that was slow in winging it.

Neither of us really cared if we brought birds home to clean and cook. I realize now how much it meant to both of us to be together as often as possible. My dad really understood what was right and what was wrong, with very few miscalculations. How fortunate I was to have him for forty-six years. He knew he was my most important mentor and enjoyed that. He made me aware that my life was my great opportunity to make decisions that could provide me with a sample of heaven or hell, without having to die.

Dad loved to travel. He believed travel was the best educator, if it was carefully planned. He trained me for years to understand the value of travel. He took me into every one of the forty-eight states at least once before my twenty-first birthday. (Alaska and Hawaii were not yet states.) Unfortunately, Dad was taken from us, but my special memories of travel with my dad have been with me every time I travel in those two newest states. I hope he knows it.

My father was a big man. It wasn't always easy for him to find the right clothes. He was also a Yankee and didn't believe in wasting his hard-earned money. Filene's

Department Store had long been known for having an excellent men's department. They also employed a unique mark-down practice. For example, if an overcoat did not sell in season, it was moved to "Filene's Basement." Once there, the price would be reduced every few days until it sold or reached zero and was given to the poor.

Dad's office in Boston was only a five-minute walk to the Basement. Dad would spot a coat he liked and then would visit the store each day that the price went down. If the coat did not sell before it reached "his" price, he would buy it. When it was totally worn out, he would consider it just right for working on his cars or in the yard. At those times, Mother would have liked to have been anywhere else! I grew up knowing that of all my friends' dads, mine was the only one who was really cool.

A SAD AND GREAT LOSS

28

My grandfather John Chase came from Lyme, New Hampshire. My mother was born in Lyndonville, Vermont. Grandfather John was about eighty years old when Mother learned she was to have a child. Her dad was a very active man. He was riding in the back passenger section of an old-fashioned people carrier in Goffstown, New Hampshire. As it slowed down, he did not wait for it to stop. He stepped off the back of the car into the path of an oncoming automobile and was killed.

It was a sad and great loss to the family. In 1926, John was well beyond any estimate of life expectancy. He was killed doing what few people his age could have done. Perhaps it was not such a bad way to end an active life. His loss meant that I never knew either grandfather. As I grew up, I felt the loss build up in my mind. My friends had grandfathers, and I didn't.

I am so thankful that our grandchildren—Sarah, Benjamin, Rachel, and Luke—have been able to know grandparents on the Perkins side of their families. Rachel and Luke know grandparents on their mother's side as well. I regret that Sarah and Benjamin were unable to know Grandfather Ranan. I wish he could be here to help me enjoy his and my fine grandchildren.

THE SEPARATION OF FOUR CHILDREN

29

Grandfather Perkins died in Nashua, New Hampshire, in 1923, three years before I was born. My other grandfather, John Chase, came from Lyme, New Hampshire. He married Nellie Lucretia Hall, one of the twelve Hall children, and created his own family of three daughters and two sons. Their home was in Lyndonville, Vermont. Alice was the oldest. She was born in 1879. Mabel was next, then Walter, then my mother Daisy Almira, and then a son, Frank Albert, who died almost immediately.

My mother was four years old when her mother died. John was training horses for P. T. Barnum's circus, which eventually became the Ringling Brothers-Barnum and Bailey Circus, billed as the "Greatest Show On Earth."

John had to separate his four children. At age four, my mother went to live with John's older brother, Adner, and his wife, Caroline Grant Chase. They had no children and lived in Lyme, New Hampshire. It was not easy for them to take in a very lively four-year-old girl who had just lost her mother. My mother stayed with them until she was twelve years old.

There was a large pile of hay on the barn floor. It was a great place to jump into from the barn rafters. Aunt Callie told her not to jump, but being eleven, she climbed to the rafters and jumped anyway. What she did not know was that most of the hay had been moved so she broke her right collarbone and her coccyx. She was in great pain but was afraid to tell her aunt. By the end of the day, she was desperate, so her uncle took her to the doctor. Her aunt became easier to live with when she realized her niece was afraid to tell her she had been hurt.

THE COW'S TAIL

30

The Root family lived in Newport, Vermont. They were a very well-to-do family with one son, Howard. As a boy, Howard spent a great deal of time at Lindsay Beach, which was owned by Howard and Alice Lindsay, who just happened to be my mother's older sister. My dad and mother visited quite often and became attached to young Howard Root. He was quite overweight. He was also lonely as an only child. I do not remember his mother or his father, but they became my dad and mother's long-lasting friends. As a very young child, Howard became my long-lasting friend too.

As a sixteen-year-old, Howard had a .22 rifle and, like so many other young boys, he tended to shoot at just about anything. They lived in the country, and there were almost no people. Howard and my dad and mother were walking down the railroad track that passed close to the shore of Lake Memphremagog. Howard was shooting at a number of harmless targets.

The track passed over a culvert with an active brook from a large pasture that emptied into the lake. In the pasture was a small herd of cows, including a young bull that had a very long tail with long black hair on its end. Howard said to my dad, "George, want to see me hit that big hunk of black hair?" My dad started to say no, just as Howard took a backward step to get a better view. In doing so, he fell off the track and dropped ten feet into that fast-flowing brook, gun and all.

Howard was not hurt because the water in the brook was about three feet deep and very sandy. Dad slid down to the edge of the brook to be sure Howard was okay. Although he was unhurt, he was wearing rubber boots that immediately filled with water and the very fine sand that was loose in the brook's rush to the lake.

With all that water and sand in his boots, Howard could hardly stand, let alone walk. Dad helped Howard get out of the brook, but once out, the problem was how to get the boots off. The wet sand had sealed all of the normal space inside the boots. The only answer was a knife, and Howard did not have one. Dad, who almost always carried a small knife, did not have one either.

At this point, Daisy arrived. She had climbed down the ten feet from the railroad tracks, and when she saw the problem, she simply reached into the case on her belt and produced her six-inch hunting knife. It was very sharp. My mother disliked dull knives. The boots were removed, and the rifle was fished out of the brook and unloaded. Howard, who lived all of his early years with the nickname of "Fat," had to walk on the stones on the track, all the way back to the Lindsays, with bare feet. And, of course, the bull never knew how lucky he was to still have all of the black hairs at the end of his tail.

Howard grew up and became a research doctor in Montreal. At one time, he owned the largest boat on the lake. When I was eight years old, he let me run that boat all the way from Newport, Vermont, to Magog at the Canadian end of the lake, a distance of about thirty miles. Howard Root is one of my fond memories of my early years. He was a dear friend of my mother and dad and me.

ROBE AND SLIPPERS

31

In 1920, their first year of married life, Mother, who was an accomplished seamstress, made Dad a wonderful lounging robe of silk. I still have it, and it is in good condition. I just can't part with it. I enjoy using things that my dad used. It lets me feel close to him.

Mother gave Dad a pair of travel slippers for their honeymoon, which she bought at Jordan Marsh. They were made of glove-soft, silk-lined leather and came in their own blue glove-soft, silk-lined leather envelope. They folded together and were flat for packing. I still have those slippers and still use them when traveling.

Dad took Mother into Boston one night, and a man made a remark to Mother. Dad hit him so hard that he never moved after he landed on the ground.

In 1946, in Tijuana, Mexico, Dad missed stepping high enough to get over a very high curbstone and badly cut his right ankle. That night he bled while wearing his slippers. He died ten years later. The ankle never healed. Doctors could not tell us what kind of germs were in that ankle. Mother cared for that problem daily until he left us.

Now, when I wear those travel slippers, as I still do, I think of the bloodstain in the right slipper that's Dad's. In Madrid, Spain, Mildred and I rented an Avis auto. We needed to photograph the Alhambra, one of the most important elderly buildings in the world. We also needed to drive to Gibraltar to visit with the famous Barbary apes, which live on that heavily fortified mountain that really is Gibraltar.

In early evening, we returned to the Madrid Avis office. We needed to change cars. It was dark in the parking area. Three young Avis men helped us repack the new car. It was many hours later, when we needed to unpack, that I realized that one small bag was missing. It was the first theft I'd had in millions of miles of travel around the world. I was angry, but it was partially my fault because I had let my watchful guard down.

My dad's slipper envelope was in that bag. I was depressed. Then I remembered that two bottles of very cheap wine and a set of very dirty underwear were also in that bag. Dad's slipper case was over fifty years old. Suddenly, I had a thought, all too rare for me. I had put dad's slippers in a suitcase. There they were! The thieves only got the old envelope, very cheap wine, and the need for a washing machine. Today, as I pack to fly to Chicago, the calendar tells me it is June 24, 2015. Those slippers of my dad's are now ninety-five years old, still in good shape, and already packed, as they should be, in my suitcase. That's proof that Jordan Marsh was a heck of a great store, and Daisy knew quality.

105 FIRST STREET

32

In 1928, Mother and Dad found the home they decided to buy. The real estate agent who had the house up for sale was Robert Stone. He was a good and honest man who became our friend after we bought our home.

Twenty-two years later, the Rotary in Melrose was trying to decide if it would sponsor my first travel motion picture. Robert was a member and was the first to vote in favor of the project. This twenty-two-year-old needed a vote, and the former salesperson provided it. The friendship would last for over fifty years.

The house was a disaster. It sat on a nice corner lot at 105 First Street in Melrose, Massachusetts. The side street was named Larabee Street and was in a nice, quiet, middle-class neighborhood. Mother and Dad had recently renovated their hotel, so having to do the same to their new home was much easier.

They tore the inside of the house apart. They put in a new kitchen, new bathrooms, and all hardwood floors. They took out partitions, closed up a back stairway that went to the kitchen from the upstairs, painted and papered, and refinished the third floor for extra space. Then they started outside. They built a two-car garage, poured a cement driveway and cement walks, surrounded the house with a one-foot high cement wall to hold in the new lawn, and planted a cherry tree, a Bartlett pear tree, and three apple trees.

The end result provided our family with a lovely, warm, and special home, filled to overflowing with love. It was a perfect atmosphere for the family's only child to develop. Dad lived there until his death in 1953, and I lived there until my marriage to Mildred in 1951. Mother lived there until 1965. She then sold the home and had a very active life until her death in 1985.

I loved living in that house. It had a big glassed-in front porch and a nice back porch, large enough to enjoy company for a summer lunch. In the summer, it was fully screened in. When the fall arrived, the screens were replaced with full windowed walls. There were three cement steps to the cement walk. Fruit trees made the fairly small backyard interesting. In grammar school, Bob Turkington, my lifelong friend, and I would pitch a tent under the apple trees and sleep outside. It was a corner lot. Dad always liked a corner lot because you could see what was on the lot from more angles. I now realize that a corner lot can make privacy more difficult.

The house had four bedrooms upstairs and an easy flight of stairs that led to the attic, which was fully finished like a fifth bedroom. When I was small, it was a great playroom. It had a small closet at one end, windows on three sides, and two huge walk-in storage closets. The house had many closets. The only negative to loads of closets is accumulation instead of getting rid of items.

The basement was unfinished but had a cement floor and was in good, usable condition. Dad had his workshop there, and when photography became an important part of my life, I built a darkroom there.

Dad put in a small steel stove so that we could burn our rubbish and have a little heat in the cold weather. One year, when I was in high school, Dad brought home some wood to burn in the stove. I was asked to start a fire in the stove. I put some of the wood in the stove, along with kindling and paper, and set it on fire and closed the top. When I came back downstairs to check on the stove, it was full of smoke but offered very little heat. I closed the cover to keep in the smoke and got some paper to start the fire again. I held the small role of paper in my left hand and opened the cover of the stove with my right hand. I lit the wooden match to light the paper, and the smoke in the stove exploded.

I was very lucky. There was just one big flash. There was no damage and no fire. I was a sophomore in high school who had to go to class for the next two months with no eyebrows, no eyelashes, very little hair, and a very red face. When Dad saw me, he was stunned. He checked on the wood he had brought home and found it had been treated with chemicals that could not be burned inside a closed space but would be fine in a fireplace. To this day, I am thankful that my eyes must have been closed at the instant that flash went off.

HIGH IN THE AIR

33

In 1930, when I was four, Dad heard on the radio that there was a huge fire in Nashua, New Hampshire. His mother and brother lived in Nashua. Mother and Dad put me in the automobile, and we dashed up to Nashua. Dashed may not be quite the right word. There were no highways back then. To drive the forty-two miles from Melrose, Massachusetts, to Nashua would take close to two hours. Dad had heard that the fire had taken almost one-quarter of the city.

There was a high wind. The homes that were burning were small, older types that were not expensive. Very little insulation was used, and incomes were small for the people who lived there. Firefighting equipment was limited, and water power was low.

We stood on Canal Street and looked across the Nashua River at the burning homes. Suddenly, there was an explosion. As we watched, a copper forty-gallon hot-water tank filled with steam crashed through the roof of one of the burning houses. It flew perhaps a hundred feet into the air, where it was caught by the high wind and disappeared from sight.

I remember my dad's comment as he looked at my mother: "It has to come down. I am glad it's going in that direction."

Grandmother's home and Uncle Harry and Aunt Delia's home were unharmed.

LOUISE FISK

34

Lewis W. and Jennie Z. Sears owned the Charlemont Inn, a very old inn located on the main highway, known as the Mohawk Indian Trail, that ran through the town of Charlemont, Massachusetts. This small town is about 120 miles from Boston and about one-half of the way to the mountains of New York State.

My dad stopped at the inn often when travel took him to the western part of Massachusetts or into the Adirondack Mountains. In the years following World War I, the early 1920s, when Dad was a salesman with the Batchelder and Snyder Hotel Provisions Company, he and Lewis Sears became fast friends. When Dad married Mother, she became close to Lewis and his wife, Jennie. One of my early memories is visiting Jennie. Lewis had died, and they had no children. I loved being in Charlemont. I remember how much fun I always had there.

The Fisk family owned a milk farm across the street from the Sears home. Their cows grazed on a rather steep hillside. I loved that farm, and the Fisk family was willing to put up with me.

When Mother and Dad purchased the Bellevue Hotel in 1923, Louise Fisk became a waitress, and our two families became quite close. Louise worked for Mother until the hotel was sold. She became a nurse, married, and had children. We remained friends until her death. She and her husband had serious health problems. Mother and I visited them a number of times, as friendship was a serious matter for both of my parents and was not taken lightly. Many of our family friendships lasted as long as life allowed.

When I was about fifteen, I was running at dusk from the Fisk farm to the Sears home for supper, and I jumped over a small ditch. Directly under me, I saw a mother skunk and five little skunks. Fortunately for me, I was running so fast the mother missed me. Dinner that night was badly in need of fresh air.

A few years later, when I was in college, Jennie Sears died. In her will, she gave me an antique settle I had admired that was in her living room and an antique bureau, which we still prize and that was used by our son George. Mildred and I have both enjoyed it. I know, without looking, that it is full. Jennie also gave me a valuable historical musket that was used in the Battle of Bunker Hill during the American Revolution. A friend of hers, whom I had known, was kind enough to give me the wonderful story of its owner. It is in excellent condition and is hanging in our family room, with its bayonet in place. The total length of this single-shot 250-year-old Revolutionary War weapon is eight feet.

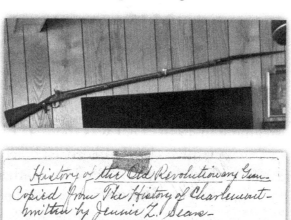

History of the Old Revolutionary Gun.
Copied from The History of Charlemont.
Written by Jennie L. Sears.

This old gun was carried by Josiah Pierce who won his fame in the battle of Bunker Hill. When the Americans were ordered to retreat he stood alone, loading and firing his gun in the face of the advancing British. When his Captain told him he *must* retreat he did so with reluctance, facing the enemy all the way, saying, "I will never have it told that Si Pierce was shot in the back." He lived to tell the story more than a half century afterward.

For "Bill" Perkins.

Copied by Elizabeth O. Potter.

MHS 1944

35

World War II was steaming in 1944. That was the year I would graduate from Melrose High School. On September 10, I turned eighteen and was ready for the draft of young men for wartime service. My older mother and dad were very concerned, and we talked about the situation many times. I believed, correctly, that the navy would ease their concerns. At that moment, my best school friend was Robert Turkington.

Bob had come to the same conclusion. His mother and dad were older too. We both decided we should enlist in the navy. We started our procedure soon after graduation, but it was December before we received our appointments. This allowed me to enter college and get in one full semester. I thought that my college should be Dartmouth, but due to my dad's health and age, I changed my mind and entered Northeastern University, right in Boston. As my life moved forward to a point that allowed me to know if attending NU was the right move, I was amazed at the huge, positive effect it created, which has lasted for my entire life.

Almost as soon as I entered NU, I was pleased to receive an invitation to attend a smoker at Sigma Phi Alpha fraternity. I gave it considerable thought. I knew I would be there for only one semester, and I needed to be serious for that time. I refused the invitation and found I had made a wise decision. By my own choice, I was not a smoker and, just like my dad, rarely drank alcohol, so I would have been totally out of place at a smoker.

I HAD IT MADE

36

I was eighteen when I started college. The war was raging in both Europe and the Pacific, and I was just young enough to miss the worst of it. So many of my friends were killed, and so many more were badly hurt in both mind and body. I wish I could understand the devastation that humans can wreak on other humans. It is such a loss to our world because war destroys the young in greater numbers than the old. War kills all ages, but youth is eliminated the most.

I remember only once when my dad showed deep personal concern, and he could not do it in person so he did it in written form. I still have that letter, and I value it beyond most of my dad's things. He was seventy-six, and for the first time he and I would be separated—completely, as far as he was concerned. I was to marry and move to my own home. He and mother knew that I had finally talked my soon-to-be wife into joining me in marriage.

When I was born, as the only child of older parents, I had it made. The three of us had great closeness and happiness. Leaving home for good was the most difficult thing I had done. It even dwarfed the agony of leaving to go to war, when the consequences could have been death or disability. To this day, I find those last few days at home were the hardest to bear.

I am sure it was much the same at my soon-to-be wife's home. Even though there were seven children, she was the closest to her mother and dad and was leaving them with continuing problems with her younger brothers and sisters.

After twenty-five years, I was taking my elderly parents' only child away from them. It was hard because both my future wife and I had deep and abiding love for our parents, and that never changed.

I DISLIKE BEING LATE

37

I dislike being late to anything. Yet I am almost always late because at the last moment, I seem to find something that I need to do that uses up the little time reserve I had set aside that would help me be on time.

My dad was never late, and my mother was of the same mind. (How could I have blown it so completely?)

On the night that I was to leave for training, the navy required me to be in Boston at the bus station at exactly 10:00 p.m. In the US Navy, being on time is a must during all training. Being late can be quite painful in many different ways. But on this bitterly cold and windy January night, Dad and Mother decided we should eat out. The restaurant they picked was in Cambridge on the Charles River, across from downtown Boston. We went to dinner early. That last family dinner was hard to bear. The war was being fought on all fronts. I was just eighteen, leaving the nest for war training.

We arrived at the restaurant at eight o'clock. At about nine o'clock, Dad was itching to get going. We all went out to the parking lot, but the car had a flat tire. Tires were not great in 1944. Dad was not happy. The wind had come up, and the temperature was close to zero degrees.

Dad and I pulled out the spare tire. Dad always had a good one. We jacked up the car and somehow changed the tire. I was in my first uniform, and my mother was positive I would damage it. Then we looked at the clock. It was now eleven minutes before ten o'clock.

Dad was driving. I do not remember any conversation until we reached the bus, less than one minute late. *Saved!* At that moment, the navy boatswain's mate in charge of our group blew up at the four men arriving just after us. It was a shocking way for my mother to be introduced to her son's US Navy experience. It brought a smile to my dad's face. He remembered how he had been in charge in Panama. (As I've mentioned, he could swear for twenty-five minutes and not repeat himself.) It scared me half to death and taught me not to be late in the navy.

There is always a good side to every bad thing that happens. You just need to be an optimist and find it. In this situation, the flat tire and tough boatswain's mate made the parting easier, in some ways, for our very close family. It was quickly over.

Boot camp in Sampson, New York, was the result of an all-night bus ride from Boston. The camp was built on the shore of one of the beautiful Finger Lakes, Lake Seneca. I learned that the lake did not freeze, due to so much water movement, even when the air temperature was zero degrees. We were trained in longboat handling on this lake, and it was zero degrees. The most dominant memory I have of Sampson is of being cold. The bunk buildings were built quickly and not very well done. There was a great deal of wind. The wind could come through any of the walls and leave in the same way. There was limited insulation.

We had to have inoculations to protect us in disease-ridden areas of the world. We were given five shots at once. I fail to remember what they were for, but I do remember the after effects. For three days, we had chills on top of our regular chills. We were so sick that all we could do was lie in our bunks and shiver. I remember wearing every piece of clothing I had: navy pants on top of navy pants. The three days ended, and then the serious training began.

On the high wall of our bunkhouse, these words were printed:

So nigh to grandeur is our dust
So close to God is man
When duty whispers low, "Thou must"
The youth replies, "I can"

During the ten weeks of serious training, several situations still stand out above all the others, even after sixty-four years. We learned the navy way with a longboat moved on water by men manning long oars on a lake that refused to freeze and in a wind that seldom stopped. This ranks as number one to me.

Ranking number two was fire control. A full-sized cement house had been built on the Sampson base that was designed to be set on fire in certain sections or all at once. The fires were fed by fuels like gasoline and oil. The wind whipped those fires into fearsome objects, with high flames and great heat. It was our task to learn how to control and finally extinguish those fuel-fed flames. I do not remember a single man who found this fun. In the real world, a few months later, we had a fire on our ship, and I remembered this training.

We were trained as a single fire fighter and as members of a fire fighting team. In the team training, one-half of the men had to advance on the fire with hoses, while the other half sprayed them with water. We were taught that fuel-fed fires are different, and they react to water in various ways. In many cases, the fires are spread by water.

I have always had a healthy respect for fire. Even with that, I am able to remember at least three times in my life when fires were threatening. Looking back, the words on the wall of our bunkhouse were true. That fire training was so hard, and we all knew it was so important that we began to repeat the words "I can," and we made it through.

The reasons for this training made us understand our possible future. At that time, the Japanese were attacking our ships with kamikaze aircraft. Their pilots were taught to fly and crash their airplanes into their targets, which were our ships. My first ship was a battleship that had been hit by three suicide aircraft. There were terrible effects and immense fires that were controlled by sailors who had fire-control training. They saved the ship.

My records held by the navy showed I was active in the rifle club in high school. It also showed that I had become a member of the NRA, the National Rifle Association, and that I held instructor status in the rifle team at Northeastern University. I lucked out. When the ten weeks of boot camp were over, I was sent to the naval air station at Pensacola, Florida, where navy pilots were trained. Pensacola was also the location for the naval gunnery training school, where I was to be trained as a Specialist G, or gunnery instructor. My duties included training pilots in the use of their weapons installed in their fighter and bomber aircraft. It was to be a ten-week course.

While in Florida, I was able to leave the ice and snow and zero-degree days behind. The change brought sunburn, very hot weather, a continuous battle with several kinds of bugs, and a constant watch for scorpions. They liked to hide in the cartons of clay pigeons we used for our machine gun training.

We always knew when a scorpion was active in the small house where we kept the clay pigeon–throwing equipment. We could hear the breaking clay pigeons as the sailor on duty tried to kill the running bug. None of us was stung, but all of us came too close for comfort. To this day, scorpions have my total respect.

During those early weeks of 1945, we did quite a bit of flying and gunnery practice at moving targets dragged by other planes. One of the planes we used had a bad reputation. It had two engines and it was an amphibian. It took off and landed on water. There were no jet aircraft. All of our planes were propeller-driven. If there was no wind, the bay at Pensacola could be as flat as a large mirror. If the sun happened to hit the bay at a certain angle, it would blind an approaching pilot trying to land, and the pilot could not tell when his plane touched the water.

If the plane hit the water at the wrong angle, it would nose over, and both engines would rip from their positions. The propellers on each engine would turn inward.

When the engines ripped off from their mounts with the fast-turning propellers, the blades would crush the pilot's cabin that housed two pilots. They would probably be killed. In most cases, very few, if any, of the passengers would escape drowning. It was a real concern because it happened too often.

All of us had to take pilot training, even though we were not pilots. We were trained how to get out of a plane that had been downed by enemy fire and was due to hit the ocean. This was the navy. We had to learn to swim at least a hundred yards in a huge swimming pool. The pool was quite deep. We also had to wear all of our safety gear and be strapped into a gunner's chair in the body of a plane.

The plane was on the edge of the pool. At a signal not seen by any of us who were in the plane, the plane would drop, nose down, into the pool. We were trained to undo our safety harnesses, release a gun housing, get out of the body of the plane while it was submerged, and swim to the surface.

I was petrified because I am not a strong swimmer. I was not practiced in holding my breath. I did not enjoy even the explanation of this ordeal as I just wrote about it here. That proves my fears were unfounded. You must do what you must do. And as Franklin Roosevelt said, "The only thing we have to fear is fear itself."

The ocean at Pensacola was very warm, and I loved it. I do not enjoy cold water. We did some fishing at night off the navy pier. Skipjack were plentiful, but they would not take bait and hook. We often saw stingrays, and one night I speared one. It was quite large. The body was three and a half feet wide. It had what looked almost like wings. It was about six feet long but about three feet of its length was in its tail. The stingray's stinger was about six inches long, and it had a series of teeth on both sides of its bone-like structure. It was incredibly sharp, perhaps the sharpest thing I have ever seen. I removed it and boiled it to remove any germs that could cause serious problems if a person was accidentally cut by it. Then I made a letter opener out of it for my father. I found out later that he was delighted to have it as a "talking gift," but he could not use it as a letter opener because the teeth were so sharp and pointed.

Our SpG rating could place us on an aircraft carrier. This meant that we had to be trained to jump from the flight deck of a carrier in case the carrier was in desperate trouble or if we just fell overboard into the ocean. With my heart in my mouth, I climbed to the forty-foot level. Navy life preservers were constructed in such a way that when you jumped while wearing one, it was necessary to cross your arms and hold very tightly to the front part of the collar on the preserver. If you did not do that, when you hit the water, it could force the preserver to rise and hit you under the chin. This could knock you out or perhaps even break your neck.

At the forty-foot level, I did as I was trained to do. I put a death grip on the front of the preserver and jumped. To this day, I cannot believe I really did it, but a navy man can do anything. The navy told me so.

Fire Control school had nothing to do with fighting fires. Fire control in the navy meant the control of the firepower of the ship. It meant the computer combined with information from all other sources that tell how to hit the target when the guns are fired.

When I finished Fire Control school, I received a promotion to SpG First Class and was sent to San Diego on a troop train. At the end of the trip, we were let out on a railroad siding very late at night. We were all traveling with our own sea bags made of heavy canvas that held everything we owned in the navy.

We were at a large base in the desert about twenty miles from San Diego. We were to remain there for quite a few days while waiting for sea duty. I pulled kitchen duty (KP). I was an SpG, peeling potatoes—and, even worse, doing hundreds of dirty dishes. There was no automatic equipment, just me and a few other guys. It was desert hot. Oatmeal was a normal breakfast. It was so tasteless that most of the bowls came in for washing with much of the oatmeal uneaten. I was up to my shoulders in cold, clammy, sticky oatmeal. The sink could hold about a hundred of those half-filled dishes. Fortunately, I had been trained at home by a doting mother. As much as I disliked what I was doing, I put things in order. I found a way to handle the leftover oatmeal, and I ended up doing a good job.

ASHAMED TO ADMIT

38

At Sampson Naval Training Center, we were all asked to give blood. I am ashamed to admit that an inducement helped us to do it; we were offered a night off so that we could go to the local town of Geneva and see people not in uniform and of the female gender, while eating old-fashioned food. Dominic Marino and I made it into Geneva twice. That is proof that we had some blood left.

Dom was from a farming family in Concord, Massachusetts, and I liked him a lot. I learned that Jane Dale, the lovely girl from Bob's band and in my class at Melrose High School, was in a college nearby. She and a girlfriend made the trip to Geneva and met us for dinner. It was a wonderful change from navy life, and it gave us a chance to show off our uniforms. Looking back, however, the uniform of a raw recruit in Uncle Sam's navy in 1945 was not a winner.

I felt very special that night. Jane had been in the high school band and orchestra with me, as well as Bob Turkington, Walter Amadon, and many others. When Bob started his little dance band, she joined as the pianist. She was an accomplished musician. I joined the band as its drummer. All the boys in our group thought they were in love with Jane. Here I was, in the navy, in uniform, having supper with Jane. Wow!

Thinking back to the band that Bob put together brings another memory for me about the navy. One of the recruits was the son of a Boston band leader. He decided the navy base needed a band, so I became the drummer. I called home to ask for my drums, my mother and dad had cases built and shipped my drums to me at Sampson. I shipped them home when my ten-week training was complete. Was all that worth the effort and the cost of the cases for the drums being built, packed, shipped, received, unpacked, used a few times, repacked, and shipped home, all within a period of just six weeks? I believe my mother thought it was worth it.

After all, I was an only child and the apple of her eye. I never dared ask my dad for his opinion.

I had been a registered NRA rifle instructor to the rifle team at Northeastern University during the one semester I completed before joining the navy. Because of that, the navy offered me the opportunity to enter Fire Control school in the navy air force at Pensacola, Florida.

Fire Control included being trained to teach pilots about their use of the guns in the navy fighter planes. It also included training in the use of 20 mm and 40 mm antiaircraft guns used on navy ships to repel attacking enemy aircraft. I accepted the offer.

While at Sampson, I learned that my dear friend Robert Turkington was in the navy and very sick; he was in the Great Lakes navy base and had almost died. He was granted a medical discharge. I also learned that Donald Tousley, another dear friend from high school, was also in the navy.

THE ANNIVERSARY DILEMMA

39

My mother and father were married on April 20, 1920. On that date in 1945, I was being trained at the naval air station in Pensacola, Florida. Luckily, I had that date locked in my mind because it was their twenty-fifth, or silver, anniversary. A few days before that date, I had been in the city and found a small jeweler who had a sterling silver sugar and creamer on a small silver tray on sale. It was just right for the occasion—except it was too expensive for me on my tiny navy training allowance.

I was about to sadly leave the store when the jeweler touched my shoulder and asked me what I could afford. When I told him, he said that was enough to buy the set. In addition, he told me he could have my folks' initials added with the date, and he could gift wrap and send it so they would have it on the right day. Dad and Mother loved it. I learned from that small jeweler how important being kind to someone can be. I have never forgotten that man. I tried to find him after the war but was unable to make contact. I regret it.

STAR SHELLS

40

We spent New Year's Eve, December 31, 1945, anchored in Inchon, Korea Harbor. I have always been glad it was my watch. My four hours started with all of the ships in the harbor firing star shells very high into the sky. A star shell is designed to provide an immense amount of light when it explodes. It then floats rather slowly back down. Try to imagine the excitement when dozens are fired at once and then continuously for several minutes. It was a fantastic, though simple, display.

The night was clear and very cold. It was a happy thing for me. My Fire Control designation gave me my watch in the captain's quarters on the ship's quarterdeck. I was alone for the four hours on a night I shall always remember.

I remember thinking about home and the way we usually spent New Year's Eve. I was only nineteen. If I was lucky and I was with someone I cared about, there would be hugs and kisses, and some of the older folks would figure into the celebration. I wrote home that night. One day I'll find that letter, as my mother saved them all, I know. It's in a small package somewhere in our attic in the small section we have not yet cleaned out.

Update: Today is April 5, 2018, and I just found them—all of them! They were carefully tied up and placed in a safe package that has been waiting for me for seventy-two years.

INCHON, KOREA

41

Inchon, Korea, was not a shore-leave paradise. The month of January did nothing to improve its already marginal conditions. We had been at sea for a number of weeks, and just being on land was beneficial. Fire control was under the jurisdiction of Chief Bosun's Mate Brueton. He had signed up in the navy four years before the war started for a four-year enlistment, and his term was up on December 14, 1941.

His ship was steaming toward the Norfolk Naval Base when the Japanese hit Pearl Harbor. Orders came through to freeze all enlistments, and the ship was ordered through the Panama Canal and into the Pacific. When he became my chief, he had been in the Pacific on our ship for over four additional years without leave. He was not a happy camper. Man, oh man, was he a salty tough sailor.

I weighed 137 pounds soaking wet. I was just nineteen when I was appointed to shore patrol duty. I was armed with a club, a .45-caliber automatic pistol, and orders, and I was sent ashore. I was a Specialist-G. I was trained to teach pilots in the naval air force how to use their machine guns and cannons. I ended up on a ship that was not allowed to fire its guns at the enemy because it carried oil to keep the planes flying from our aircraft carriers. The *Cimarron* was one of five ships that proved to be one of our secret weapons that the Japanese never understood. They could not understand why our carriers never had to sail into a port to refuel. Our five tankers would fuel the carriers while both ships were traveling at twenty-two knots, an unbelievable ability.

So here I was, all 137 pounds of me, doing shore patrol duty on the docks of Inchon. I had a short break to look over the town. Another SP man and I walked through the town, and up on a hill, we saw a church. It was made of stone and appeared to be Catholic. We climbed up and found that it was open; in fact, there was a service going on in Korean. That was the first time I ever saw holy water.

Somehow we ended up in the service, and I was given a taste of wine and bread. I believe that was the first time I had ever had communion. I felt, at that moment, as if I needed it.

Except for being cold, all went well at the docks until we saw a sailor coming at a dead run. He was being chased by a very angry and large Korean. We shoved him into a boat and set it free. Then we paid attention to the Korean man who'd almost caught our sailor. He was boiling mad. It seems he had caught our sailor paying attention to his daughter. It was not the attention that bothered him but the type of attention. He cooled off once he understood who we were and what we had as duty. It was the only real problem I experienced during that duty. It was Tokyo where the duty was more complicated.

NITRATE FILM

42

In December 1945, we were anchored in the harbor of Inchon, Korea. It was a very cold, very damp, very windy, and totally inhospitable place—not a place that we could enjoy very much. It was a place where a lot could happen that we would like to avoid.

The *Cimarron* (AO-22) carried motion pictures that could be shown to the crew when needed. Some were training films and others were old Hollywood productions that we all had seen a number of times. The Mess, a perfect name for our dining area, had a small built-in film projection room at one end. It held all of our reels of film, projectors, and other equipment. It was an all-steel-plate room. It had one steel door to enter and exit, and a small steel window that could be opened when it was time to project the movies.

In 1945, nitrate film was still in use. Nitrate film is dangerous because it is highly flammable and can explode under some conditions. The sailor who was the projectionist saw the film starting to burn and leaped out the open door (or hatch, as it is called on a ship). He slammed the hatch closed as he had been trained to do. That one quick move probably saved him, the ship, and all of us on it.

For the next hour and a half, the ship was under maximum fire-condition rule. The steel plates of the projection room became bright red from the intense heat. We were sitting on a ship that was loaded with one hundred thousand barrels of diesel fuel. No one was allowed to smoke on the ship, except in one small location on the outside fantail (stern or back end of it), and even that was with fire prevention in place.

The fire remained contained in the projection booth. If we had let it get out of control, it could have sunk the ship with all of us on it.

It was so cold that seawater was beginning to freeze on the outside deck. We had formed a bucket brigade. When the ship was loaded with fuel, the main deck was only about four feet above the water line. When the fire alarm went off, we ran to our duty stations, even if we were in our underwear.

If we were caught that way and the water was freezing, it could be a hard nut to crack. Some sailors were stationed at the railing on the main deck, dropping buckets into the harbor water and pulling them up full. Other sailors were handing them to the next sailor in line. A second line of sailors were handing the empty buckets back. We poured hundreds of gallons of seawater onto those red-hot steel plates.

The smoke was toxic. The hose men were passing out from the fumes because they were inside the hull of the ship. The bucket men were moving in clearer air. Most of us were in dungarees and shirts, and we were so concerned we did not have time to feel very cold. Our fear was that the fire would spread. Even the deck and overhead were red-hot. The fire had to be fought on the deck above and below the red-hot room.

We were able to retain the fire and keep it from spreading. When the real danger had passed, we were all surprised that we were covered with ice. The battle was won. When the steel door was finally cut open, we saw that everything in the room had melted from the intense heat.

THE WIND PICKED UP

43

On the way back to our ship, the wind picked up, and the sea became increasingly dangerous for a loaded longboat. Water began to accumulate in the longboat, and the extra weight pushed the longboat deeper into the sea. It soon became apparent that with such a large cargo of paint and with the increasing waves washing over the boat, it would soon sink. We all were wearing life jackets, but if we were forced into the ocean, some of us would not be found.

Decision: Heave the darned paint. We did, and the boat floated. We made it to our ship, and the longboat was hoisted aboard. The doctor in charge made us line up, and each one of us was given a drink of cognac. (A few thought about going for more paint but did not do it.)

Being my innocent, mother-protected self, I had never had cognac. I saw the men taking it in a gulp, so of course I thought that was the way to do it—and I did it. I could not breathe. I gasped. My eyes watered. I choked—and I made a head start on my new naval-hero reputation.

To leave one ship to board another, my sea bag was tossed over the deck railing to the waiting longboat that would take me to my new quarters. I then made it down the rope ladder and into the same boat with my sea bag. I settled down into the bottom of the longboat and started talking to a sailor who was perhaps ten years older than me. I was taller than he was, but he had "salt on his shoulders," which meant he'd been a seaman for a long time. I learned he was a merchant seaman on the northern Murmansk course. He had been in the northern ocean twice, and both times submarines had sunk the ship he was on. Life expectancy, if you went into the northern ocean, was about fifteen minutes due to the temperature of the water.

When we arrived at the *Cimarron*, she was partially empty. The height from our longboat to the open first deck was about eight feet. We started to board. The sea bags had to go up first. When it was my turn, I stood up shakily because the longboat was rocking. I picked up my sea bag and, like everyone else, threw my sea bag up eight feet to the main deck.

Unlike everyone else's bag, my bag did not make it. I grabbed it again and swung it up with all my strength. Again, it dropped back into the boat. I heard a voice say, "Oh, for C—— sake, get out of my way." With that, the smaller seaman grabbed my sea bag *and* his and heaved both of them at once up onto the main deck. Then he climbed up the ladder and held his hand out for me to grasp. My reputation was growing rapidly. I will never forget that day or that seaman.

A PRETTY YOUNG WOMAN, SHIRLEY ANN

44

In October 1945, I was on a hospital ship anchored at Eniwetok in the Pacific Ocean. I met a sailor who lived in Gardner, Massachusetts. He dropped a photograph of a pretty young woman on the floor. I picked it up and asked him if it was anyone special, and he told me it was just a friend. I did not have a girlfriend that I was in touch with, but I wanted to have one to write to during the many dull moments that occurred on any naval ship at anchor with no place to have shore leave. I asked if he would mind my writing to her, and he said, "Heavens no. Here is her address."

That night, I wrote my first letter to Shirley Ann Singleton. A few weeks later, I received my first letter from her. In May 1946, while at home on leave, my dad drove me to Gardner to meet her. We arrived at her folks' home and were invited in. She was upstairs. Her dad called to her, and she started to come down the stairs. Let me illustrate the power of a uniform. She saw me standing there with my dad, called my name, rushed down the remaining stairs, and greeted me with a wonderful, tight hug and kiss. My day was made! My dad was all smiles, and her dad seemed not at all sure how he felt. Her mother was barely smiling.

We spent the afternoon getting to know one another. She was a working model with the Roly Rogers agency in Boston and was a year younger than me. Our friendship blossomed. I went back to finish my time in the navy, and in September we dated a few times. She found that she could fit into my spare uniform, and we had our picture taken together. After a few dates, we agreed on a brother/sister relationship. It lasted until her death sixty-one years later. Her children are also my friends.

GROW A BEARD

45

My first year in the navy at the age of eighteen was a very interesting life experience. I was so young-looking that I felt the need to look older was a necessity. It seemed to me that every sailor was older than me. I needed to change this, so I decided to grow a beard. After all, I was shaving but not very often.

Six months later, my ship was in the San Pedro navy ship repair center near Long Beach, California. I had a day and night off, so I went in to Los Angeles in the early evening and decided to see a movie. I found a theater; the film was a horror movie called *Dr. Cyclops* (or something like that). I was feeling pretty salty. I was in my uniform, wearing my service ribbons, with my easily combed beard, and I had reached the age of nineteen.

A pretty young woman came in and took the seat beside me. We became very friendly, and when the show ended, we went out together. It was a promising situation. We decided to drop in to a cocktail bar in a local hotel. We were walking along, holding hands, when she suddenly stopped short. She looked at me for a moment and then said, "I don't believe it. With all the sailors in LA, I had to pick up the only virgin in the United States Navy."

That was proof that my beard did work. But darn it, my dad's advice stood between me and choosing which kind of fun I should have. I was still a virgin on the night Mildred married me, and so was she. We learned a lot together. My dad was right: You do not have to die to experience great joy.

I just had a thought: How did that girl know?

WHAT DO YOU MEAN, A "DRY STATE"?

46

My wartime service ended on July 13, 1946. I was ordered to leave San Pedro Naval Base in California on a troop train for the city of Boston, Massachusetts, for formal honorable discharge. I was delighted, until I found out about that train. It was a very warm time of year in California. I knew it would be hot in every state we passed through on that seven-day/seven-night journey of over three thousand miles. I learned that our train used a steam engine that burned coal. The cars where I would be living and sleeping had no air conditioning and were at full capacity. The bunks used for sleeping would double as seating in the daytime.

The steam engine sent its hot exhaust smoke from the burning coal over the top of the troop-filled cars. All doors and windows for air had to be kept open both night and day, making it difficult to breathe. There were moments when the war in the South Pacific had almost comforting memories.

A bright spot appeared on the third day, when we learned we would be stopping in Kansas to recharge our engine's supply of water. We learned we could get off the train and enjoy solid ground for over an hour. Many of the most active and thirsty men made a grand plan of action. An hour would be enough to leave the train and run to the nearest ice-cold service store. There, they could stock up on cold brews and stronger aids to help keep sanity strong on the hottest days and nights.

The dream was almost at hand. The train was now stopping on a siding, and the landlubbers began to pour huge amounts of water into the engine. The carefully laid plan was started; the chosen men took off at a dead run for the nearest supplier of ice-cold beverages with high-proof status.

Only then did they find out that Kansas was a dry state.

My computer cannot handle the agony that the runners carried on their way back to our travel haven. I fear it would melt.

THE WEAKER RAT

47

The US Navy had five fleet oilers named for rivers in the United States. My ship was named the *Cimarron*, fleet number 22, and had a crew of about 250. All of the gyros, which tell the captain the degrees of balance for the ship, and control units ended up in our office. We were deep inside the ship and had duty twenty-four hours a day. There were four of us, so we were able to divide our duties and work time and still have the pleasure of some privacy. We moved our bunks into the fire control space. It was that situation that trained me to be able to sleep under almost all conditions and to go to sleep quickly. The gyros and equipment could be very noisy.

It seems that rats enjoy living on ships, even US Navy ships. We had more than our share, as we were in the warmer waters of the South Pacific. If you were sleeping on the top bunk of the three-bunk–high units and any pipes were over your head, there was a very good chance that a rat would be walking on that pipe while you were asleep. If another rat was coming from the other direction, they could not get by each other. This would probably cause a pushing problem. The weaker rat would probably fall off the pipe and land on the person asleep in the top bunk—a great reason to be in the fire control office, where we slept on cots.

It got so bad that the medical office offered fifty cents for every rat that was captured, dead or alive. The sailors' pay was thirty dollars a month, so trap lines were very active. One day the odor in the fire control office became unbearable. What could it be? We tried all day to locate the source. Finally, we focused on a steel plate on the floor. We loosened it and raised it and found a few dead rats under it. The rats had taken a liking to the wrapping on some of the electric wires. Once they chewed through it and their teeth hit the live wires, they were dead. The temperature stayed close to ninety degrees. Need I say more?

In the famous China Sea, where storms have caused many a ship to sink, we were attacked by a major typhoon. We were a ship that was designed to withstand any kind of weather, but we were about two-thirds full of fuel, so the main deck was about eight feet above the normal water level. In that typhoon, which lasted over twenty-four hours, the ship had to head into the storm. The major waves would hit the bow and pass over the length of the ship. At that point, the water on the main deck would be over thirty feet deep.

Fire control had to be in touch with the bridge and the captain every fifteen minutes for the entire twenty-four hours. We had a gyro to tell us the degree of pitch the ship was experiencing at all times. We came within four degrees of the point at which this huge ship was in danger of tipping over. It had never come so close. After about eight hours, the telephone between control and the bridge gave out. For the rest of the storm, we had to carry the information to the bridge. It meant wearing a harness and rope to keep from being washed overboard. We took turns. All four of us had to make the trip once an hour. It was the longest twenty-four hours any of us had ever endured. Finally, it was over, except for the memory that is vivid, even as I write.

WE DON'T HAVE TO TELL YOU EVERYTHING

48

The AO-22 was one of America's secrets in World War II. The Japanese could not understand why the US aircraft carriers never had to refuel by going into a port. It was because five fleet oilers loaded with one hundred thousand barrels of diesel fuel were able to keep up with task force movements and refuel the carriers while both ships were travelling at twenty-two knots.

A fleet oiler could visit a port or base, fill its tanks, and not attract any attention compared to a giant carrier. The fleet oilers in a task force were under orders to avoid doing anything that would attract attention. They were well armed but not allowed to fire their cannon if in a task force. If their fuel tanks were full, the ship was safer than when the tanks were partially empty and filled with explosive fumes.

One of the tankers was sunk in the Battle of the Coral Sea by being machine-gunned by a Japanese aircraft. It is believed that one 20 mm cannon in the plane fired one round that pierced a partially empty fuel tank that exploded. I was told that the ship sank in twelve minutes, with the loss of all of its 255 crew members, but I have never seen this in print. We were aware that it could happen to any fleet oiler, so all of us were very careful to follow our book of rules.

ELAINE BRATCHER

49

San Bernardino, California, is an hour or so from Los Angeles. When I was there in 1946, the mayor was a man my folks knew from Nashua, New Hampshire. We visited him and his family. Later on, when I went back to LA on business, I stayed at his home. The actress Dorothy Lamour spent time living with them. I used the same bed she had used (but sadly, she was not there at the same time that I was).

Harry James, the band leader and marvelous trumpeter, and his wife, Betty Grable, were neighbors. She was a famous pin-up queen during the war years in the '40s and on into the '50s. I enjoyed my stay with the Nashua folks very much.

While in the navy, I went to the Alhambra High School to look up a friend. I met a pretty young senior whose name was Elaine Bratcher. I was in uniform, and that helped. I ended up taking her to her senior prom. Her being with a sailor in uniform made an impression on her friends. We enjoyed our time together, and we dated a few times when I was able to get shore leave. During this period, my ship was in the San Pedro repair facility next to Long Beach, twenty or so miles from Los Angeles. Elaine was studying voice and doing very well. I remember the day she was asked to sing "The Star-Spangled Banner" at a professional football game, and she received an ovation. Her father was an executive at Chrysler Corporation and took us all out to dinner one evening. I learned later on that he and her mother had divorced. Her mother was in the real estate business. When my time in the navy came to an end, I went home to Boston. We were friends and stayed in touch.

After my time in the service, I went back to Northeastern University. Elaine called and told me she was coming to Boston to visit. It should have been happy news, but it wasn't. Elaine was a talented and warm young woman, *but* I had met a girl, Mildred Boyle, who was a senior at Melrose High School, class of 1947.

I have never known how to handle Mildred in some situations. In this case, I had only dated Mildred for a short time. But even then, her chemistry had me in hand. Elaine was coming to visit and was to stay at my home. We were fond of each other. I was twenty years old, and my hormones were wide awake and active. Mildred was already a major factor in my life, but I didn't understand it. I could not date Mildred while Elaine was staying with me. Elaine was a year older than Mildred. That one year, at that age, was a serious consideration. Like an idiot, I debated for about three and one-half minutes on taking them both out together. I didn't think I was serious with either one. Then why did I keep trying to call Mildred while hiding in our first-floor closet with a telephone that could reach that far? I guess I really was hooked. I have always feared making Mildred unhappy. If tears should develop, I was a wet dishrag.

It turned out that Elaine was pretty serious about me. I enjoyed her feelings, but she lived in California, and I was really enjoying a relationship with a girl in my hometown. I nearly lost Mildred. I finally found a way to see her, but Elaine was still here. I called a friend, Fred Blue, and he and I began taking Elaine around. At Revere Beach there was a large roller coaster. I had a terrible fear of heights, so Fred took Elaine on the coaster. I ran for a pay telephone and called Mildred. It was hell.

I did not want to hurt the feelings of either girl. When Elaine left, I knew it was over because Mildred had become so important. To this day, I feel remorse for not knowing how to handle such a situation. I was just weak, I guess, when it came to doing the right thing when it involved two girls.

COUSIN OF CARMEN MIRANDA

50

Don Pedro Todd was a cousin of the actress Carmen Miranda. She was popular in the 1940s and was known for her huge and colorful hats, many of which included fruit and flowers. I have happy memories of comments my dear father came up with regarding those partially edible hats.

Don Pedro lived in an apartment in Long Beach, California, about twenty miles from Los Angeles. I can't remember for sure how I met Don Pedro, but he owned a big two-door Lincoln automobile that impressed me. Our ship was being repaired in the San Pedro naval base, so I was able to be off the ship quite a bit. It was early spring of 1946.

Don Pedro disliked driving, but I enjoyed it. I hadn't driven for close to two years while in the navy, so the chance to drive that big Lincoln was just great. Don Pedro and I traveled quite a few times together. The time I spent with Don Pedro remains a bright memory, even after sixty-three years.

Friendship can have many difficult moments. How much value friendship brings with it depends upon how each individual perceives it and values it. To me, friendship means a great deal. One day we were very late returning from a distant location. Don Pedro suggested that I stay overnight, and I agreed.

Don Pedro made a late supper for us, and then we sat outside on his balcony. Don talked about the huge tidal wave that had hit Long Beach many years before. When it was time for bed, we shared it, as there was only one. It was an important learning experience for me because my good friend was gay. I was nineteen, with no experience that prepared me for that situation. It was highly educational. As soon as Don Pedro understood my feelings, he put friendship ahead of his personal inclinations.

Don Pedro remained my friend until his death many years later. In 1946, when

Mother, my dad, and I were in Los Angeles, I called Don Pedro and arranged a luncheon. We all met, and my folks handled the situation with great skill and appreciation for his friendship and kindness while I was so far from home in the wartime navy. I have given much thought to how Mother and Dad would have reacted, had my relationship with Don Pedro blossomed. My parents were realists. They would have been shocked and saddened over never having any grandchildren, but they had been forced to adjust all their lives. They would have accepted my situation, and it would not have changed their love for me.

I believe that the way you believe and the way you choose to live is no other person's business. It is your life, and as far as we know, you will have only one.

A last thought has to be this: I hope that you may be blessed with good judgment and that it will bring you happiness, love, and friendship.

ONE OF THE KINDEST MEN

51

One of the kindest men I have been blessed to know was Harry Beckwith. Harry was older than my father and very successful. When he was young, he conceived the idea of building a steel-box toe in work boots to prevent injury when heavy objects were dropped on workmen's toes. When he received a patent on this concept, it made him a multimillionaire.

Harry's office was in the Statler office building in Boston's Park Square. He lived in a wonderful big home in Rye, New Hampshire, and owned the Farragut Hotel next door. He also owned the Wentworth by the Sea Hotel in Portsmouth New Hampshire.

In 1956, the Beckwith Arden Corp., owned by Harry, had about two hundred employees. There was no retirement age, so the average age of his employees was sixty-seven. Harry believed that if you could get to work and wanted to work, you had a job, no matter how old you were. I asked him if I could bid for the group life insurance plan, and he agreed to let me do it.

John Bradley was Provident Life and Accident's group specialist. He was a very dear friend and was extremely smart and honest. We made up the bid. It became the highest cost per $1,000 ever written in the Provident due to the average age of the employees, but it lowered Harry's insurance costs substantially.

When I went to see Harry in his Boston office three months later, I envisioned that the big group case being canceled, and I cringed. That was not the case at all.

"Do you know who had that group policy before you?" he asked. "It was my son-in-law. He deserved to lose it because he wasn't on top of it!"

I nearly had a heart attack.

In Boston, the Algonquin Club on Commonwealth Avenue is about as blue-blood, proper Bostonian, and expensive as you can get—and hard to join. Harry

111

invited me to lunch there and made sure we sat with other top business executives. It was his way of helping me to expand my horizons. He introduced me to his friends, all presidents of Boston department stores, manufacturing companies, and research groups. It was quite a heady experience.

Harry hated to drive, but my dad loved to drive. My dad retired in 1946 at the age of seventy and was in good health. Harry was still working every day at nearly eighty. He asked my dad to drive for him. They really liked each other, and Dad was delighted. Harry would call Dad and say, "Could you pick me up on Wednesday? You have the Cadillac at your home. I need to go to the Wentworth. We can have dinner there." Dad was always ready. Harry would call again and say, "George, I'm taking the train with my wife. We are going to stay at Pinehurst, and I plan to play as much golf as I can manage. My clubs are in the Cadillac. Could you drive the car down and meet us there next Sunday?" Dad would be expecting this, and he would be ready to leave as soon as the call came in.

Then there was the time Agnes McKinnon, Harry's longtime housekeeper in Rye Beach, called for Dad. Agnes was in her seventies. Harry and his wife were moving to Florida for the winter, and she needed help with closing up the Rye house. Dad said he would help her. Mother heard him talking to Agnes, and when she found out what was going on, she called Agnes herself, as they had become personal friends. She asked Agnes if she could use some additional help, and Agnes was delighted. When I heard about it, I offered to go too. In the very large reception area of the Beckwith home, on the middle of a huge glass-topped table, there was a marble copy of Rodin's *The Kiss*. I would have enjoyed owning it.

I have always appreciated fine china, glassware, linens, handmade rugs, and well-done paintings and bronze castings. Harry and his wife must have enjoyed entertaining, as they had over two hundred complete place settings of china, crystal, and sterling silver, which required a very large storage area when not in use. They were absolutely beautiful. We also had a chance to enjoy the rose garden at its best.

Dad had to give up being with Harry when he was about seventy-seven. Harry had asked him to drive a full carload of sterling silver from Rye Beach, New Hampshire, to Harry's winter home in Florida. The weight of the silver was in hundreds of pounds. Dad made it okay and then drove back home to Melrose, Massachusetts. Serious driving was almost ended due to his age.

For a number of years Nashua was the home of the Melville Shoe Company, purportedly the largest in the world. Harry was also involved in the creation of the Thom McAn shoe company. My whole family used Thom McAn shoes for years.

In 1946, Harry sold the Wentworth by the Sea Hotel to the Smith family. The mortgage was difficult for the young Smith family to manage, so Harry held the mortgage until they had proven they were capable and hotel winners. Because of Harry and our friendship, I spent many happy hours photographing that grand old hotel, with its tidal swimming pool and its gardens, tennis courts, and extensive facilities. I loved their dining room and the food available there.

Every year Harry invited his family to a Christmas party at the Algonquin Club. He knew I had just completed a serious study of the Mayan Indians of the Yucatan in Mexico. He asked me if I would show my film at the Christmas party, and I was happy to do so. Everything went very well, and the family seemed happy and interested. As I was leaving, Harry put an Algonquin Club envelope in my pocket. When I arrived home, I found $250 in the envelope! Back in December 1950, that was serious money.

MY TEENAGE YEARS

52

My teenage years hold very few memories of conflicts with my mother and my dad. We, as a family of three, were very close in many ways. Mother was a businesswoman, used to earning a living at a young age, and Dad held a very demanding position as a chief purchasing agent for the state of Massachusetts. He was up and out by seven o'clock each morning and home by six thirty and very tired. By my tenth birthday, my growing allowance depended upon having the garage doors open for dad's arrival each night.

It was easy being with them. Most of the time their requests made sense. I was so comfortable with them that it was easy to follow their leads. They, in turn, seemed to understand the trials and tribulations I was facing as I entered school and had young friends. Dad was a lover of travel, so we were on the go much of the time. My first visit to Bermuda was at age four and a half. Canada followed at age five and continues to capture my interest and enjoyment, with extensive travel in that grand country throughout my life.

Perhaps the largest contributor to my satisfying life has been the ages of many of my dearest friends. Early in my life, most of our family friends were around the same age as my parents. They were very warm-hearted, sharing, storytelling men and women. They brought such fascinating ideas and happenings to the attention of my parents, which also included me because I enjoyed being with them. That surprised them.

LADY SOMERS

53

On Friday, April 11, 1931, Dad and Mother took me to a great wharf in Boston, Massachusetts. I was four years and seven months old when the three of us boarded the Canadian National Steamship Company's RMS *Lady Somers* to sail to Bermuda. It was my first travel by steamship and my first visit to a foreign land. (I'm amazed that I have memories of that trip.) I saw a giant whale for the first time, breaching not far from our ship. My dad and mother were more excited than I was, so I guessed I should get excited too. Whales have given me pleasure a number of times since then, and they excite me now just as they excited Dad and Mother back then.

In Bermuda, I saw horses, which excited me because I had such great memories of my adopted cowboy grandfather, Dick Randall. Back then, Bermuda required travel by horse and carriage. Only a few emergency motorized vehicles were allowed, not at all like it is today. It took the horse a little over an hour to take us to our hotel. By the time we reached the Elbow Beach Hotel, I was very sick. I was having a hard time breathing and was very uncomfortable. Mother asked the hotel for a doctor, and they rushed us to the doctor's office. He examined me and told us the very bad news from my point of view but not as bad for my folks.

I was allergic to horses. Riding behind that horse in the open carriage had done it to me. I had what the doctor called "horse asthma." He said not to worry, but he wasn't me, a blossoming cowboy. There was no cure at that time, so I had to be kept away from horses as much as possible. I had no idea how much that problem would affect the rest of my life. I have always loved horses, and now there is medication to control the asthma, but it was a long time coming.

The Elbow Beach Hotel was much larger than the family's Bellevue Hotel that was my first home. It was high above a pink-sand beach and the ocean. There was a small band playing in the dining room. Our waiter knew that I had started drum lessons, and he told the band leader, who then came over and invited me to sit in as the band's drummer. I did, but it was just for a few moments. From little things big things can grow; it works. The last time I was in Bermuda, the old Elbow Beach Hotel was there in name only; it was all new except for its name. Logical after eighty-five years.

The Crystal Caves in Bermuda were fun. Our guide through the caves stopped at a deep pool of water. She told us it was eight feet deep, and to show us how clear the water was, she dropped a large pin into the pool. We could see it on the bottom, and the water seemed to enlarge it a bit. When we came out of the caves, we had lunch.

The little restaurant had a pool of water perhaps ten feet across. In the pool were many rather large groupers. There was a piece of rope with a knot on one end, and the other end was tied to the railing that surrounded the pool. You could pay a small fee to drop the rope with the knot into the pool. The fish were so hungry they would fight to grab the knot. If you could pull the fish out of the pool, the restaurant would cook it for you, and your lunch for the family would be free. My dad asked me if I would like to try, and of course I said yes. The fish was so strong that it nearly pulled me into the pool. The rope burned the skin off my left hand, and I still carry the scar. Dad paid for our lunch.

Bermuda was my first travel experience with my dad. I learned how important travel was to him. He believed it was a great educator if you absorbed all that you were seeing for the first time and learned to watch for changes every time you revisited each place. During this first travel with dad, he showed me how to sightsee and really make it worthwhile. There was no simply looking out of the car windows and asking about everything I saw. Bermuda opened the door to a future life filled with world travel and adventure that would continue into my elder years and continue to educate, just as my dad believed. (Thanks, Dad.) I've found that he was right in the ways he taught me to think about life and living and the wonderful values of friendship and family. I was a very lucky kid.

FORTY-FIVE ARROWS AT THIRTY YARDS

54

Mother and Dad both came from average families, but both had a strong desire to grow mentally as well as financially and were not afraid of hard work. They were capable, smart, honest, and focused, and they grew together. They were very good for me.

When I was four years old, we visited Governor Alvin Fuller's wonderful stables in Rye Beach and North Hampton, New Hampshire. Dad had a wonderful work ethic and gave his employer a clean, honest effort every time. When he retired from the purchasing position he had handled alone for twenty-five years, it took three men to keep up his responsibilities. I remember when Governor Fuller told him that his was the only expense account that went across his desk that he did not question. One of the Fuller horses, whose name was Nashua, ran in the Kentucky Derby.

I'd been wearing a little gold ring, and when I got home, my mother saw that it was missing. Two weeks later, Dad had occasion to visit the Fuller farm again, so Mother and I went along. As we were walking along a path, Mother saw something glitter. It was my little gold ring that I had lost two weeks earlier.

Mother believed that idle hands were the basis of much trouble with children, and she made very sure that didn't happen with me, to the point where I would have enjoyed a breather! At age four, I started drum lessons with the Mont Music Manor, and both Frances Mont and Retta Wilson believed as my mother did. (Looking back, that may be where I first heard the comment "Out of the frying pan and into the fire.")

When I was six, Miss Mont gave a concert in the old town hall in Lynnfield, Massachusetts. I performed my first public solo on the stage upstairs. When I finished and was enjoying the applause, I went to sit down, and the little girl behind me pulled a "Charlie Brown and Lucy" on me; she pulled my chair back, and I sat down on the floor—to even more applause.

That day I learned an important lesson that has helped me in many different situations. I learned that people like to laugh, and if it happens to be at you, it can be very valuable if you have learned to laugh at yourself, to the happy surprise of those around you.

Mother also believed that I should be interested in competition, and when I was eight, she had a wonderful elderly gentleman, who was an expert at building the bows and arrows used by the best archers, build a set for me. When I was nine, the wife of Mr. Frentz and a national champion archer became my instructor. I became the youngest competing archer in the country for one season. By the time I was ten years old, there were two other nine-year-olds, and I was old hat.

In July 1935, I was entered into a shoot—forty-five arrows at thirty yards for young archers. The poundage in the pull on my bow was twenty pounds and required a great deal of effort. Mrs. Frentz had also entered me in a repeat of the morning effort in the afternoon. I should have withdrawn from the match, but somehow I completed the course. That night I became quite ill. I had pulled twenty pounds forty-five times in the morning and then the same in the afternoon, a total of ninety arrows on one very hot July day.

I could not reach to pick up anything for two days, and both of my shoulders were swollen for nearly a week. I did learn that, at times, it is possible to do the impossible if you set your mind to the task. I also learned that there is a time to stop what you are doing when and if conditions have changed.

Mother also enrolled me in Mrs. MacAnanny's dancing classes before I really knew what a girl was. The classes were fun, and the girls gradually became more interesting. When I was eight, the little girl who lived across the street and was about twelve became interested in a medical career. She needed to study anatomy and decided that I should be the patient. She was a good student and studied hard several times. I was several years older before I was able to be the doctor, but it was worth the wait.

HAPPY CHILDHOOD

55

After returning from a cruise to Bermuda, many small health situations started, beginning with finding out about my allergy to horses. My first year of formal education began in Miss Willey's first grade class in the Melrose Winthrop School on First Street. This was about a ten-minute walk from my home at 105 First Street.

On September 10, 1932, I turned age six, just in time to enjoy looking at Miss Willey, who was very pretty. Once in the first grade, the horse asthma caused breathing problems and a number of other minor illnesses that prevented me from attending classes. This caused me to repeat first grade.

My mother was so upset; she told the school that I would not be returning. She did a massive search for a private school that would enable me to take first grade and second grade combined. She located a private school whose principal was a Miss Sowdon. Due to my health situation, Miss Sowdon said she could arrange to educate me with all the requirements for the first and second grades combined. It was totally successful.

Our beloved Dr. Pike in Melrose determined the need to remove my tonsils. The date was set for January 24, 1933. It would be done at our home. Ether would be given to me while I was in bed in my room. He would then carry me into the kitchen, where the kitchen table would be ready for the actual removal to take place. As I write this, I remember the sound and the impact that each drop of ether made as it landed on the facemask I was wearing.

MRS. GEORGE WILLIAM PERKINS
105 FIRST STREET
MELROSE, MASSACHUSETTS

1-24-1933

This pin Bill held in his hand as
means of protection from the Doctors
when he was to have his tonsils
out and he confided in me and
gave it to me in case I needed
to use it

Bills mother

P.S. I want to add that Bill was a
soldier never made a struggle and he
wanted mother to hold his hand and such
confidence and mother did and stayed
with him as he wished

Love is Blessed

MELROSE, MASS.

This is for Bill
as a sovereign of his youth
I would like to add
Love like this was a blessing for your mother

121

I spent the second through sixth grade in Miss Sowdon's private school. When I was eleven, Miss Sowdon decided that I should study French. For some reason, I was the only one to whom she decided to teach the language. She couldn't speak it, so we had a very trying fifth-grade French class.

Miss Sowdon was from the old school method of teaching, which I had a good chance to see firsthand. She believed that if a child was not behaving, the child should be told to stop. If the child did not stop, then it was up to the teacher to make sure that the child knew he/she was in the wrong. She was an expert with a ruler. She could hit your knuckles and never miss. When I was twenty-three, I saw her for the last time. I went to visit her one-room school and had a happy reunion. Her dedication to teaching and attention to detail taught me well.

It was seldom that a parent would object to her using the ruler, but my mother and dad did not believe in that kind of punishment. I had a few spankings but only with my mother's hand. My dear mother decided that the best way to discipline me was to put me off by myself, with nothing to play with and away from all the activity that was being enjoyed by others.

I will never forget the times that I acted up at the dining room table when there was company. Mother would march me to the downstairs half-bathroom. She would sit me down on the seat (with the cover down, of course), and she would tell me that I was to stay there until I decided I could be good. I would stay there alone until I could not stand it any longer. Then I would call, "Mommy!" When she came down, I would tell her I was sorry and that I would not do it again. Then I would be allowed to return to the table and join the company. That always seemed to work. I never misbehaved very many times before I understood that it was easier to be good. I didn't like sitting alone in that little bathroom with everyone else having a grand time. It was a good way to calm down a child. I really had a comfortable life.

When I was thirteen, I played with Earl, another thirteen-year-old boy, fairly often. One day when he was alone, he was bitten by a dog that had rabies. Back then, many dogs never received rabies shots as they do today. Earl had to receive a series of shots into his stomach area, which he said was very painful. When my mother was a young girl living in Lyme, New Hampshire, a grown man contracted rabies and died in agony. It made a lasting impression on her. Rabies can prevent you from being able to swallow. You become very thirsty, yet you cannot drink anything. It sounds horrible, and I have been conscious of the disease ever since.

Mrs. Huxford was the teacher of my eighth-grade English class. We all had to learn a poem and recite it in class. I had just spent a lot of time on Grandfather Randall's ranch in Montana. I learned the words to a cowboy poem and recited it in class. My classmates loved it.

I thought one day that just for fun, I'd see how cow punching was
done;
So when the roundup had begun, I tackled a cattle king.
They saddled me up an old grey hack, with two setbacks on his back;
When I got on, he spun around and I fell off and hit the ground
and had
One hell of a fall!

Mrs. Huxford sent me home for swearing.

While still in the eighth grade, I decided to wear my bright-red cowboy shirt to school. The teacher took one look at that distracting shirt, and off I went to the office and then was sent home. At last I was establishing an image. I had sworn in school and shocked the teachers. I was on my way!

My father left all of the discipline to my mother because he did not have the patience that my mother had. My father never hit me, not even once, but I wasn't really bad very often.

When I was fourteen, Mother and Dad decided I was too sheltered and sent me to Camp Medomak in Washington, Maine, for two summers. The first night, six of us went to our tent to sleep. It was the first time any of us had ever spent the night away from home (and in a tent in the dark). Suddenly, we heard a terrible scream and then more screams. Somebody was in very bad trouble. We all pulled the blankets over our heads, but it didn't help a bit. Then the first flashlight was turned on, and we thought we were brave. Then more screams. We weren't.

We made it through the night, and in the morning, our counselor asked us if we had heard the screams. We all played it cool. He told us we would get used to it. Families of loons called to each other often at night. I learned a lot, although I was homesick. I had to do my own laundry, and I missed Connie Jenness, my first girlfriend.

There was a canoe-carrying contest. We had to hoist a fifteen-foot wooden (and very heavy) canoe onto our shoulders and carry it quite a distance, over and around objects. Due to the weight, position, and balance problems, I did a lot of private practicing. One of the older canoe people taught me how to properly carry the boat, and I won the contest. It was exciting!

Every year the camp had a Parents Day. We boys showed our visiting parents samples of what we did each day. I am sure Medomak was eager to prove that the money our parents paid was worth it.

One of the activities for Parents Day was a dunk tank. A chair was carefully set up over a large tank of cold water. A round target with a black center, about six inches across, was connected to the unit holding the chair. For a small contribution to the expenses of the day, people could obtain tennis balls and try to hit the target.

The most important part of the whole arrangement, however, was finding a parent who was willing to sit in the chair.

Mr. Robie, one of our neighbors and a very nice man, was a very successful businessman. I remember many talks with him and about him. He was the owner or primary investor in one of the early new automobile rental companies, like Hertz. He was visiting his son and offered to sit in that chair—he was the only parent who offered. He sat, fully dressed, in that chair and was dunked five times. No wonder his son was proud.

On the final day at Medomak, I was packed, ready to leave, and waiting for my mother and dad to pick me up. Right on time, my dad drove into the yard, where many of the boys were waiting. I would remember this day for the rest of my life. Out of the auto came Connie Jenness with a kiss and hug, and all seen by my competition. I was the only guy with that perfection in plain sight of all. We held hands most of the way home.

Interestingly, Camp Medomak is still in operation today, although there have been many changes.

"FORE!"

56

When I was fourteen years old, I somehow got hold of a golf club and a golf ball. It was the first time I'd ever held a golf club, but I went out on our front lawn, put the ball on the grass, swung back the club, and hit the ball. I watched that little white ball sail high into the sky. It went completely over the Masons' house that was across the street on the corner of First and Larabee Streets. I ran up First Street, trying to find my ball.

Three houses up, I saw our neighbor, Mr. Craigie, resting in his front yard. I stopped and said to him, "Mr. Craigie, did you see my golf ball?"

He looked up at me from where he was lying and said dryly, "Is that what hit me?"

The ball was nearby, and apparently it had knocked Mr. Craigie out colder than a fish. He was a small, slight man, about fifty years old. He had several children and was very good with kids.

When it dawned on me that I had hit him with my golf ball, my first reaction was, *Wow, what a drive I made! That ball went over two houses!* Then I realized I could have killed Mr. Craigie. He never said a single unpleasant word to me; his only comment was, "I could be dead." Both Mr. Craigie and I were very lucky, and I decided to forego a career as a golfer. Bob Turkington was with me when I hit that ball. I never saw Bob hit a golf ball. That one try was enough for both of us.

MONT MUSIC MANOR

57

When I was a freshman in high school, I met a girl who lived next door to Walter Amadon, one of my closest friends. I was petrified of her because she was so pretty. Her name was Jean Carlton, and all of my friends liked her. One day I asked her if she would go bike riding with me. I was amazed when she agreed and got her bike. I had never really dated at that point. We went riding, and somehow I ended up stopping at my house to introduce her to my dad. It was my only "date" with Jean, but she remains a delightful memory.

Mont Music Manor was a skillfully managed place to learn about the musical instruments used in the Melrose High School orchestra and marching band. Frances Mont was in charge of the Melrose, Massachusetts, high school music. Retta Wilson and Mrs. Wing were both piano teachers. I was their student for about one year. My only regret is not continuing with the piano. It is marvelous to be able to sit down and play the piano. What a great way to get on with your life. However, when I decided to stop piano lessons and concentrate on percussion, both of my piano teachers were delighted. I wonder why?

Miss Mont was an able instructor on a number of instruments. I studied percussion—drums—with her for over eight years, from the age of four to age twelve. I also enjoyed the high school band and orchestra for all four years. Lasting friendships began at Mont Music Manor.

I studied art for a number of years with George Wing, Mrs. Wing's husband, who was a fine artist himself. I really enjoyed his private lessons, learning to use pastels, oil paints, and charcoal. He was my friend for about six years.

Jane Dale was a beautiful girl, a skilled flute player, and a fine musician. All of my friends wanted to date Jane. She dated us all a little but none seriously.

Bob Turkington was a very fine cornetist (similar to a trumpet). He started his own dance band, and I joined as his drummer. We kept it going for about three years and played locally quite often, but when the war came, most of us joined the armed forces.

AT THE AGE OF EIGHT

58

On my fifth birthday, Dick Randall called me to say happy birthday. He also reminded me of his promise to me. About this time my music teachers, Frances Mont and Retta Wilson, were visiting the first great national park, Yellowstone. They were staying in the Old Faithful Hotel, near the great geyser with the same name. Their room was on the third floor. While they were in their room, they heard a great commotion. They opened their bedroom door just as a black bear climbed over the railing of the fence that kept guests from falling off the third-floor walk. They slammed their door. Regrettably, the park rangers had to kill the bear.

Seventy-six years later, in 2007, I visited the current manager of the hotel and asked him if he knew about that incident that had happened so many years ago. He was amazed. He told me that he had heard about it but could not find any record of it happening. He was delighted to know that it really had happened.

When the great forest fires hit Yellowstone in the 1980's, they came within six hundred feet of destroying that wonderful old hotel.

At the age of eight I got my first two-wheeled bike. My best friend Bob Turkington lived close by and got his first bike at the same time. We were out riding on the cement sidewalk near my home when he tossed me a stick that I could not catch. It went through the spokes in my bike's front wheel and stopped the wheel from turning. That made the bike stop instantly. I went over the handlebars and fell on my face on the edge of the street's curbstone. When I hit the ground, the sharp edge of the granite curbstone broke the inside corners off my two new front teeth.

Bob and I went home. When I walked into my mother's kitchen, she took one look at my bleeding mouth and started to cry. She knew that my teeth could not be repaired, and I would have to live with two broken teeth. Bob disappeared but was back in a few minutes. He had gone to where we had our accident and had searched for the two broken corners of my teeth. He found them, brought them back, and gave them to my mother, asking her to glue them back on. My mother was so touched by what he had done that she stopped crying and accepted the accident's result. I, in turn, found out that I could eat an apple easier and faster than any of my friends because my two teeth were now pointed. When I was nearly sixty years old, my brother-in-law, Dr. Lawrence Boyle, a wonderful dentist, was able to back up the two teeth and make them look perfect for the first time since I was eight years old. I still have those two tiny broken corners that Bob found. I value them.

I remember one other interesting moment with Bob. My mother could not stand having a dish that was nicked. She had a house helper by the name of Jenney Blanchard who was very hard of hearing. (The old saying was "deaf as a codfish"; why, I do not know.) Jenney was very careless when handling my mother's dishes. When my mother would complain, Jenney would say, "Just buy a new one." It would really bug my mother, but she put up with it because Jenney needed the work; because she was deaf, it was hard for her to find a job.

On this particular day Bob was on his way to my house. He was walking up the path to our back door just as Mother found a favorite cup that Jenney had badly nicked. It was one of the very few times that I can remember my mother really flipping out. Just as Bob got close to the three cement steps my mother, using language seldom heard in our home (except for Dad), opened the back door, and threw that nicked cup down onto the cement steps as hard as she could. In that instant, my friend Bob was gone. It was quite a while before he dared show his face at my home again.

Bob and I remained close friends. We both married and had children, and our wives became friends. During World War II we both served in the navy. Bob became very ill in boot camp and nearly died. I was there when he and his wife, Jean, celebrated their fiftieth anniversary. He died shortly thereafter. I lost a very dear friend, but his wife has continued our friendship.

AMAZING STORY

59

This is the amazing story of a twelve-year-old child who loved the travel pictures by Burton Holmes, shown in person every year at Symphony Hall in Boston. He went with his dad and mother and two friends, Dow and Cristina Hicks, from McKees Mills, New Brunswick, Canada, who also loved to travel. It was always dinner, parking, especially good seats, exciting travel-minded audiences, and then Burton Holmes in his white tie and tails. His clothing, his voice, and his name correctly pronounced, as used in the places shown on the large color movie screen, were so very special, but it was most of all the man. Lowell Thomas said he was the finest man he had ever known.

Holmes created the word *travelogue* and was considered to be the world's greatest traveler. He brought his travelogues to the largest audiences for sixty years. He loved the National Geographic Society and Constitution Hall in Washington, DC.

Fourteen years later, in 1952, that child, now a young man of twenty-six and associated with Burton Holmes, was presenting his own "Burton Holmes Travelogue" to a sold-out house. He narrated his own motion picture travelogue that he'd created with his friend Lowell Wentworth, its great cinema photographer, titled *The Four Seasons in New England*. It has been rated the best two-hour film ever made on our home location, mainly, I believe, because we used all four seasons.

When I approached the podium, I found an unopened envelope waiting for me. It was from Burton Holmes. The writing on the envelope included my name, speaking at Constitution Hall, the address of the Hall, the date, and a note that asked to have it on the podium, unopened. With that huge audience and the National Geographic people waiting, I took a deep breath, opened the envelope, took out the paper, and read what was a letter to me. The letter was from Holmes at his home in Hollywood, California, announcing his retirement. The letter asked me to tell the audience the following: "Thank you for being the most distinguished and most appreciated of all his sixty years of world-travel Burton Holmes Travelogues audiences. Thank you."

Being asked by Burton Holmes to voice his retirement message to his favorite and most important audience and our National Geographic Society was one of my most important lifetime moments.

THAT SLINGSHOT

60

The third floor of our home in Melrose, Massachusetts, was a perfect place for me to play alone with all of my private thoughts and ideas. Normally, Mother knew what I was about to think before it took place. She was a project-minded person who was always ready to tackle almost any new thought, just to have the fun of finding out if it could or would work out. I remember the way her mind worked and things she was involved in, and I think that may be part of the reason why I developed into a project person myself. New ideas were there, even when I was twelve, if not even a bit earlier, often causing me hard-to-answer questions and several that demanded her special form of retribution.

A friend had a slingshot that could throw a small stone a very long distance. If the stone was round, it would go farther and faster than a misshapen one. Small stones also went farther than heavy stones. It was fun learning about such choice items. I had a small tube of BBs. I don't remember where I got them, but they gave me a great idea!

That slingshot was very heavy to carry around. The elastics that gave it its strength were hard to find. They had to be replaced in a difficult way, being tied into both sides of the handle and tied into both sides of the small leather strip used to hold the stone for throwing.

I had one of my mother's wire coat hangers. I knew where she kept a pair of wire cutters. I also had a small piece of white leather—very soft, flexible, and easy to trim with Mother's scissors. I had a lot of strong elastics from the school library, and I had time. It was Saturday, so I made my own slingshot.

Made it! It worked! A BB was perfect! I could not believe how fast and how far it would fly! All it needed was accuracy, and with loads of immediate practice

I learned to be deadly. Sneaky, too. That slingshot was so small it would fit in my pants pocket.

There were three windows on the third floor of our house. One looked down onto First Street and the others looked down on Larabee Street. Our home was on a corner. I found the single window was very easy to open, and there was no screen. The third BB I shot hit the front window of a passing auto. It apparently disturbed the driver, who came to a screeching halt and leaped out of his car, looking everywhere for a suspect. No open windows anywhere.

O'DONNELL SCHOOL

61

My dad always remembered his first through sixth grades of school in Nashua, New Hampshire. The grade school was named for the Reverend John O'Donnell, who was a member of the school board in Nashua and a very respected man. The school took his name at his death in 1882. Over the years, the school was used less and less until 1936 and finally closed. My dad heard from a friend that the O'Donnell School was being put up at auction by the city of Nashua. By this time it had been empty and unused for a number of years.

Dad was interested in purchasing the school. He remembered the good times that he had when the population was very small. He called the city to learn the date of the auction and decided to attend. A very hard rainstorm started just as the auction was getting underway, and Dad was the only person who showed up to bid. Dad purchased the school building in its elderly condition for $1,500.

After taking ownership, he realized the amount of work necessary to simply clean out the empty building. One of the first things he did was to find the small chairs that were his when he was in the sixth grade. The little chairs were bolted to the floor of the classroom. I remember him undoing the bolts on the bottom of each chair. We still have both of those small chairs in our family.

Over the next three years, Dad and Mother, with the help of friends and family, emptied, cleaned, and converted the school into eight apartments. The apartments were rented on a weekly basis, as incomes in Nashua were small for the average person. It was a profitable ownership, and the building was retained for nearly sixty years.

Recently, I took pictures of this old building, which has been completely renovated by the new owners. The value of the building is now over $300,000 and is still being used for apartments.

DOROTHY REED, THE ACROBAT

62

Dorothy Alice Reed was a little girl who lived in Newport, Vermont. She was wonderfully limber. If I called her double-jointed it might explain how remarkably she could control her body. At the age of ten, her mother was taken from her in a terrible accident. Dorothy had been studying dance since she was four years old, and her skills were already well developed. The last request her mother made to her father was to be sure that her daughter continued her dancing education.

The first time I saw this girl dance, I remember how beautiful she was. I learned we were both twelve years old, though she was a few months older than I was.

Her dance was unforgettable, and she moved her body into positions that seemed impossible to me. (She also was able to drink water while sitting on her head!)

I was lucky that I was able to spend much of my summers for several years with my aunt Alice Lindsay at her beach home on one of the most beautiful lakes anywhere, Lake Memphremagog. One-third of the lake is in Vermont and two-thirds in Canada. The summer that I was fourteen, I learned that Dorothy was dancing at the Barton Fair, a few miles from Newport. A friend and I hitchhiked to Barton. Dorothy danced with so much skill and grace, and she was so beautiful that I fell head over heels in love.

There were times when Dorothy would work for my aunt, cutting up fruit that was served to the paying guests who spent their vacations at Lindsay Lodge. I remember her commenting that the task never seemed to end. My aunt served her guests well, and the quantity of food she prepared would not be forgotten. One night, a bunch of us kids came in from the movies in Newport, all hungry. It was fairly late, and my aunt was asleep. My aunt had made many pies for a luncheon the next day, and they were just sitting there. When my aunt came into the kitchen in the morning, the pies were mostly gone. The large party was scheduled to arrive for their luncheon in about four hours. My aunt instantly knew where the pies had gone, but she loved us kids, and not one angry word was spoken. She went to work and made all new pies, and somehow was ready for her guests. Aunt Alice was a very special woman who had many trials and tribulations in her life, but she was able to survive all of them. We all loved her.

The next summer I was back at my aunt's. Dorothy was there often. My friend Don Tousley visited. He was touring on his bike. Don was the kind of fellow who was able to do many exciting things, like skiing on top of Mauna Loa in Hawaii—on snow, no less. Virginia Light was a friend of Dorothy's. She was very pretty and blonde. The two girls and us two boys were riding our bikes to ride into town when a big guy in an automobile forced us off the road. I don't remember what the problem was, but, like kids might do, we tried to hide in the long grass of a hay field. It didn't work; he found us, and we thought he was going to become physical, but all he did was yell.

At sixteen, I learned how important it was to have someone that you could care deeply about. My first date with Dorothy Reed in Newport, Vermont, changed my life. She was tall, about five feet nine and a half inches in her sandals. Dorothy had great courage. Her dancing lessons were in Montreal, Canada. It was a two-hour train trip from Newport to Montreal each way. She made that trip alone as a very young girl many times.

My dad told me, "Life is made up of many situations. Try to have happy and productive ends to each one. You are a very lucky young man to have Dorothy interested in you. It is your responsibility to take good care of her. This is a good example of what I told you. It is a time when you may need to make decisions. Remember you do not need to die to have heaven or hell. Protect that girl from your own desires. It would be very easy to make her life difficult indeed. It would also open the door to hell a lot wider for you."

It was difficult at age sixteen. Then it really became a challenge at seventeen. At eighteen, my mother became the manager of Dorothy's dancing presentations at various clubs and situations. She was always with Dorothy. She had an eagle eye on that girl, and that included me. It made it a little more difficult for us because at that time, Dorothy was living with us. Each time I came close to the decision, my dad's advice got in the way. I knew he was right. I did not fail him.

Dorothy and I were separated by World War II. She joined the USO and danced for the troops in Europe and especially in Italy. I joined the navy and served in the South Pacific. Just before I left home for the navy, Dorothy gave me a silver ID bracelet that read "George William Perkins." On the back of the bracelet she had engraved my navy number, 8048270, and her initials. The war ended when we were both twenty years old. She went on to dance in New York City with her own success, and I went back to college. In the end, we both married wonderful partners and have enjoyed our lasting, lifetime friendship. My dad understood what a managed, thoughtful, and love-filled life was all about.

Dorothy later chose a husband wisely, had four children, twelve grandchildren, and six great-grandchildren, and to my pleasure, we are still friends. I still wear the silver name bracelet she gave me when I joined the navy.

I am telling you this so you will realize that if you handle relationships correctly, you can have friends for a lifetime. This lady from Vermont danced her way into entertainment history, traveled, withstood the trials of competition on the New York stage, and never lost her soft-spoken Vermont accent or her gentle ways. A few years after her marriage, she went to nursing school and graduated as a registered nurse. Even in 2008, at the age of eighty-two, she still was giving her time in the care of hospice patients.

COLLEGE TIMES ARRIVED

63

College times arrived. Dartmouth College in Hanover, New Hampshire, and the University of Massachusetts in Amherst, Massachusetts, were beckoning.

With Dad's advancing age came diabetes and failing eyesight and hearing. I knew that I soon would be in the service and away, so I chose Northeastern University because it was close to home and had a good co-op program. I only had time for my first semester before joining the navy.

In 1946, I returned from the service and returned to Northeastern. I purchased a decent 35 mm camera and took Mother to Quebec City, Canada. I photographed the old city, came home, and put together a slide show for the fun of it. I showed the pictures to a few small groups and loved the applause I received. I was twenty years old, and a new dream was fermenting in my brain. I loved going to Boston to the Burton Holmes Travelogues at Symphony Hall, as I had been doing since I was twelve. My parents always purchased season tickets for us.

Northeastern offered a wonderful approach to higher education. The co-op plan allowed students to go to class for a thirteen-week semester and then work on an approved job for thirteen weeks. It would take five years to obtain a bachelor's degree. During that period, students would have enjoyed considerable on-the-job experiences with a single company or perhaps several companies, and because they were earning a paycheck, it helped with the costs of a full-time college education. There was a good possibility of graduating with a permanent position all in place.

The first co-op opportunity for me in 1946 was at the home office of the John Hancock Life Insurance Company, with whom I still do business. While working there, my interests in photography developed. In 1947, I knew that I would need a promotion to let people and companies know that I existed. My major was in marketing and advertising, and in 1948, I asked Dean Melvin to allow me to create my next co-op position myself. He let me try.

Early in 1948, the Renault Automobile Company of France was attempting to introduce the smallest four-door sedan in the world to the American public. Their best dealer was the Charles Street Garage in Boston. The most difficult roadway in North America was the war-built Alcan Highway, from Dawson Creek in British Columbia to Fairbanks, Alaska, a distance of 1,523 miles on terrible dirt road. If the "little Toot" as we referred to it—weighing 1,200 pounds, costing $1,200, with four doors, a partially air-cooled motor, and averaging forty miles to the gallon—could make it, it would really interest a large segment of the American public.

My marketing idea was a three-month–long road test from Boston to Fairbanks, Alaska and back to Boston, a distance of 12,500 miles. My co-op job would be to make the test. Glenn Whitham, president of the Renault dealership in Boston, had to be sold, as the cost would come from the factory and his dealership. I was successful. The story of that three-month test tied to the co-op plan is great fun and highly educational. It was a great career starting point. Dean Melvin was a wise man.

I hold the all-time record over the Alcan Highway in several categories. One is 5,500 miles of dirt road in one trip. I also hold the record for paid speaking engagements on travel: 146 in 143 days while driving 44,000 miles.

OVER THREE MONTHS

64

On our 1946 coast-to-coast automobile trip, we decided to visit Tijuana, Mexico. At that time, it was a small country town in a country that time had almost forgotten. The population of the United States was less than one half of what it is today. San Diego had grown due to the war in the Pacific and the city's wartime efforts. Little Tijuana was pretty quiet. Most of the streets were unpaved. It did have some curbstones that were higher than normal by several inches. Dad tripped and racked his shin on one of those high curbstones and cut his ankle quite badly.

In just one night, infection set in. That was in 1946, and dad died in 1956. Mother took care of that poisoned ankle for ten years, but it never healed completely. No doctor who looked at it could find the right way to treat it or a correct medical name to give to it.

Lowell Wentworth and I spent over three months studying and filming the wonderful country of Mexico. We heard that in the far southern part of the country, there was a town called Juchitan. It appeared to be quite close to the border of Guatemala. We were told that it was unique because many of the management people were female. We decided that it would be wise to see for ourselves if such a condition could exist in a male-dominated country like Mexico. We were filming in the historical city of Oaxaca, and Juchitan was only a day's drive farther south.

When we arrived, we drove through the open market and saw almost no men working in the various shops. The costumes women wore for various functions were very beautiful.

There was only one hotel, and we learned that the manager was Wilber Barker, an American. That was good news. It would save us time and effort in finding out if our information was correct about the position of women in business and in the city government. Lowell and I ate many meals at the hotel, and we became very friendly with Wilber, spending almost a week with him.

Our waitress at the hotel's restaurant was about thirty and a pleasant, rather substantial lady. Lowell was tall, slender, light-haired, and very good company. When our waitress served Lowell, she often used her elbow to jab him rather hard. Lowell asked Wilber why the waitress kept giving him her elbow because it was actually painful. Wilber said it was because she really liked Lowell. Wilber also told us that she was actually nearing the age of forty and had already buried one husband.

Wilber had lived in Juchitan for over twenty years. He had married a native woman and was quite happy. We found that the mayor and the prosecuting attorney were both women. We also learned that many of the men were at home caring for the children. The women really were different from any other part of the country.

WENTWORTH BY THE SEA

65

By the time I was twenty, I knew that world travel and photography were my dream. My dad and Burton Holmes had opened the door a little wider. In the summer of 1946, Jim Smith and his wife purchased the Wentworth by the Sea Hotel in Rye, New Hampshire, from our dear friend Harry Beckwith, and they saw my pictures of the hotel. Jim asked me if I would take the pictures to a union meeting in New York City. The union was trying to decide if they should hold their large meeting at the hotel in the fall. It was a challenge that I could not turn down. Jim made the arrangements, and I took my photographic color slides and drove to New York.

The meeting was held at the world-famous Waldorf Astoria Hotel on Park Avenue. I was delighted when I found that I would be a guest for the night after the presentation was over. I made certain that I would be on time. I located the room where the Union was to meet and was surprised when I learned there would be about forty members making the important meeting-location decision.

The room was all set up. It contained five round tables with eight comfortable chairs at each table. In the center of each table were four unopened bottles of a very expensive 100-proof liquid on a beautiful round tray. About an hour before the dinner, three members of the union arrived. I let them know why I was there, and they acknowledged that I was expected. They allowed me to make arrangements for the projector, and the hotel had already set up a screen in a good location so all could see.

I learned that I would be the last speaker at the meeting before a vote would take place. I was asked to leave before the vote was made so I would not know the result.

The meeting started but I was not in the room yet. I was to come into the meeting room at a given time. This was all new to me and was not what I had expected. I was growing more nervous with each waiting minute.

The great moment for my entrance finally arrived. As I walked to the podium where I would explain the joys of a meeting at the beautiful Wentworth, I noticed that all of the liquor bottles on each of the tables were now open. In fact, I tried to see one that was still unopened without success. As I looked at my audience, I had difficulty finding anyone who was not under the influence to whom I could explain the many good reasons to meet at the Wentworth. The pictures went over very well with the half dozen sober members able to see them. I had become an entertainer of a group of people who did not know I was there. I was getting educated in this type of public speaking.

Late the next day, I met with Jim at the Wentworth. As I walked into his office, he rose to his feet from his desk and said, "Congratulations! The union just approved having their meeting here, and they said you made a wonderful presentation. The vote was unanimous. Thank you."

May wonders never cease.

FONDNESS FOR MEXICO

66

In 1946, I spent a number of days renewing my fondness for Mexico. Dad and Mother had learned to appreciate that lovely country as well. We visited there for the first time in 1939, driving many miles on some rather difficult roadways, but the gentle people more than made up for the roughness.

At the age of twenty-one, I was feeling the excitement of that age for men. I tried to dance the Rumba at El Patio with disastrous results. The embarrassing moments traveled with me for several months after returning home. Suddenly, a thought broke through my youthful memory that was positive. I had been a member of the Learn to Dance school owned by its dance instructor, Christine Jensen MacAnanny. I had endured [and sometimes enjoyed] the agony of learning how to ask new young girl members of the dance school to dance with me at a time when I hardly knew how to dance myself.

When I was nine, my dear mother believed strongly that any hour I was not trying to learn something new was a wasted hour. She began to sign me up for various activities starting at age eight to be sure I would be ready for age nine, but age nine on up into high school required dancing instruction.

Mrs. MacAnanny seemed surprised when I called and explained my disaster with the Rumba in Mexico. She agreed to give me private lessons to ease my apparent distress, so we set the time and place. It was at the same location as in high school. When I walked into the studio, I saw someone standing near the door. Who could that be in a silk print dress with long brown hair and a certain way of standing that brought her shoulders slightly forward. I realized she must be a dancing school aide, of course. But that girl? It was impossible for her to be there to dance with me, but I looked around and realized I was the only student! I could not believe my luck! Hubba, hubba; I was home! Her name was Mildred Boyle, no middle name. If she should marry, Boyle would become her middle name. It was later on in my life with this delightful creature that I learned whispering "hubba, hubba" into her ear that night almost cost me my future, not to mention my life!

Soon after we met, I was away for a month taking pictures of big-game hunting in the hell-roaring section of Montana. Mildred wrote to me. That was in 1947, which was a year of terrible forest fires across the United States. Our friends the Dennisons lost their summer home in Gloucester, Massachusetts, and our friends in Maine suffered greatly

In 1948, with college and financial leanness, we continued to date, but her folks thought she was too young to be serious, as she was only nineteen. Although she may have been willing to marry, it did not work out. I was too stupid to make my move, so we delayed joining forces. Looking back, it was the loss of my early life, those two lonely years without her.

In 1949, Bob Dow and I went to Alaska to road-test the little French Renault. We were gone well over three months. It was very hard on Bob and me to be away that long, but it was very lonely for Mildred. A chill runs up my spine when I think of how close I may have come to losing her! (During our second year together, things kind of faltered. I was ready to get serious, but she and her parents were not!) She started dating her boss in a silkscreen company where she worked in Cambridge. He was smarter than me, drove a vintage Rolls-Royce, came from a substantial family, and was *very* attentive. Mildred told me that he took her to a special restaurant to hear Vaughn Monroe, a very popular band leader at that time. I nearly died! I had no money and even had to borrow my dad's car. Talk about competition! Then she told me that we were breaking up! I couldn't stand the thought. In all of my life, those weeks of separation were the worst I can ever remember. I could not stay away. I tossed pebbles at her bedroom window and tried to see her every way I could find. She went to a party with him, and I took a girlfriend of hers. When I saw them together, all I could think of was winning her back. Finally—praise all the powers that be—she dated me again.

As soon as I mustered up the courage and felt the time was right, I proposed. She refused. I proposed a second time, and this time her dad refused me! She refused me a third time, but I was persistent! Finally, while I was on my knees in the living room of my family home at 105 First Street, she accepted. My future life was saved.

DEAN MELVIN OF NORTHEASTERN UNIVERSITY

67

Dean Melvin of Northeastern University was an understanding and, I believe, wise man. He helped me on my co-op decisions and functions that made his college famous. As I've mentioned, my first co-op opportunity was the home office of the John Hancock Mutual Life Insurance Company in Boston, Massachusetts. That company was active with the co-op program of Northeastern. I accepted the offered clerk position in the commission office of the company's Group Insurance Department. The pay was thirty dollars a week. It was a valuable experience for me and introduced me to the life of working for a giant corporation.

First of all, my being accepted was based on my completing a work application. The young lady who helped me fill out the application was Nancy Concannon. She did her best to be helpful, and she was successful. I have always remembered her as a rather special lady. I found the work in the Group Department to be somewhat boring, but it had its moments. Part of my duties included checking the commission statements paid to many of the group-insurance sales agents for the policies they were selling.

One of the checks that came across my desk stood out above all the others. I had never seen a check anywhere near as large as it was. It could not be right. I took it to my supervisor, who agreed that it was abnormal, so he decided to check it out for me. An hour later, he called to tell me that the amount was correct. It was six figures and was the commission on a new case. The agent had redesigned the entire group-insurance package for one of the largest automobile companies in the world.

That moment in my life created a major change in how I looked at just about all business situations. Even today, I still can see that check and hear the words, "The check is correct."

I began enjoying being a part of the John Hancock family. They were building a new home office. A statue of John Hancock would be in the lobby. The employees were able to contribute to the cost of that statue in an effort to make all of us feel as if we were involved in the great new project. I remember that I donated five dollars. To this day, I am glad I did.

I also was enjoying my first camera. I was able to find places that would pay a small fee to have special pictures displayed. During a week's vacation, I drove to Quebec City and took many photographs. It was a start in my dream of world travel. The John Hancock magazine did an article on me; it was my first. The cover of this business publication and its story about a clerk in its Group Division helped me make changes in my future life that I could not have imagined. Think and become rich. That sounds good, but think and enjoy life sounds better to me. I showed it to Nancy Concannon, although I'm sure she doesn't remember. Her approval of my job application so that it could move forward was an important, kind moment provided by a stranger.

I have believed for many years in the combination of college and actual work. It did well for me and for many of my friends as well. I had been in co-op work at the John Hancock for about a year. It had a few problems, like all businesses do that have people working for them. I enjoyed every hour I put in. I enjoyed the people I was with every day. The company made it easy to have needed breaks. Continuing education was available to any employee who looked forward to personal growth and advancement if the employee wanted to stay with the company long term.

One day there was a notice on my desk that there was a meeting for employees, and I was expected to attend. No one seemed to know much about it. It came at a difficult time for me, but I decided to attend anyway. When I arrived at the meeting, I was told I had to sign a statement saying that I was very much in favor of an outside union. I didn't know what an "outside union" was, so how could I sign a paper saying I was in favor of it? I learned that the person I was talking to was a union organizer. He let me know that I was creating a problem for my future by not signing right then and there.

That did it for me. The next day, the people with whom I enjoyed working were up in arms over a union situation. They wanted to know how I felt. I was almost twenty-one. I was still frosted by the comments the organizer had made to me the night before, and I told them so. Over the next several months, more organized union meetings were held. I learned what I would have to pay to be a member. I learned about striking and forcing the company to change in the way the union ordered. All I could see was that organizer and the way he ordered and warned me. I guess I was very outspoken against the union attacking the John Hancock.

My supervisor came to me one morning at nine o'clock and said that I had been asked to attend a meeting of the board of directors of John Hancock at eleven. He didn't know why. He didn't know if I was in trouble, but he did know that no junior-level clerk in the Group Department had ever been called in before. At ten minutes before eleven, two vice presidents arrived to show me the way to the board meeting on the top-executive reserved floor. Why me? I was co-op and twenty-one.

I was taken to the private office of the executive vice president near where the board was meeting. It was a beautiful office. A pleasant young woman welcomed me and knew that I was nervous.

"You'll like Judge Byron Elliott," she told me. "I'm his private secretary. Would you enjoy coffee or perhaps tea?"

Mother was a tea drinker, so I made big points when I told her that tea would be delightful.

A slender man entered the office around eleven thirty. The pleasant young woman stood up at her desk and said, "Judge Elliott, this is the young man you sent for. His name is George Perkins. He is working in the Group Department. He is also here on the co-op program with Northeastern. He enjoys tea."

Judge Elliott came over and greeted me with warmth and a solid handshake. The only way I can explain my first reaction is to refer to the physical chemistry that draws people together. I could not have known how important this meeting would be to my future, but a friendship was born at that moment that would last until Byron's death.

Judge Elliott asked, "Would you be willing to answer questions asked by board members?"

"What kind of questions?"

He answered honestly. "The basic questions could focus on the union efforts to move into the company, and perhaps some might be on unexpected subjects."

I agreed, come what may.

With my limited experience in business and certainly feeling that my job was most likely at stake, I followed the judge through his personal entrance into the board room. About twenty men were seated around a huge, magnificent table in very comfortable chairs. A great amount of paper was in front of each man, along with many coffee cups and water glasses, most quite empty.

Judge Elliott introduced me as a co-op employee who was in his second year working in the Group Department. He mentioned that he was aware of my outspoken objections to the unionization battle that the company was enduring and that I had agreed to answer questions asked by any member of the group. He did not introduce each member to me because a fancy name holder sat in front of each man.

Their many questions covered many subjects that usually focused in some way on the subject of the union efforts. I tried to be brief and focused with each of my answers. When I was asked what would I do to make the company less at risk, I went deep into my memory of nearly two years at the company, and I made the following suggestion:

"During my two years at John Hancock, no senior executive of vice president level has been to our department. There is no friendly relationship between top brass and the daily workers, who actually keep the company going. The big brass is out of sight and taken to be unfriendly. I suggest that all of the senior executives should put into their schedules to visit the 'little folks' as often as possible and be on a first-name basis, easily helped by all of the supervisors. The company is really a great company but internally not very friendly at high levels."

The judge thanked me several times during that meeting. He then invited me to have lunch with everyone in the board's private dining room with its very classy uniformed staff and special menu.

This amazing man took me aside about six months later. "I've read the story in the company magazine about your travel and photography interests," he told me. "You should do your best to have a great life. If you ever would like to come back to work at the John Hancock, there will be a position waiting for you."

I was almost overwhelmed by having this great senior executive take his time and be interested enough to offer guidance to a college student like me. In the next years, after I left John Hancock to sow my own oats elsewhere, the judge would meet me, and we would go to one of his clubs for lunch once each year. The year the company built its Chicago home office, I was waiting for him in his office to go to lunch. His private secretary was still with him, and we were friends. He was never late. But on this particular day, he was about thirty minutes late.

He was now the president of the John Hancock and came in all apologetic. He shook my hand and said, "Today I have made the most important decision in my business life. I have been under great pressure for more than two years to build the world's tallest building in Chicago. It would be over a half mile high. Today I refused to build it. I could not live with that high a building on my conscience. Let's celebrate at lunch." And we did.

He was a great, kind, and gentle man and my friend. Years later, I did want to rejoin the John Hancock, so I called the judge. He invited me in for a conference and told me to talk with every vice president of every division and pick the one I would like to work in. He was also a man of his word, and he believed in promises.

I have never forgotten how I was treated by this man and have tried in every way to carry his way of helping another person into my way of living.

BIG-GAME HUNTING

68

In 1947, Lowell Wentworth and I were filming *Big-Game Hunting in Montana*. We were staying at the ranch home of Bill and Helen Randall on Mission Creek, enjoying Mary Lynn, their little three-year-old daughter, while learning what life was like on a working cattle ranch.

A few months earlier, I had been really lucky. I had met the kind of girl dreams are made of. Bill Randall was very good at making beautiful designs in leather. The way he could decorate a saddle was remarkable. He also enjoyed creating western-style leather belts. I could not stop dreaming about that delightful creature back in Boston, and Bill needed relief. He told me to stop drooling, and he would make me a beautiful belt to take home to her.

It was a great idea, but a beautiful belt would need a western buckle. I decided to hitchhike into Livingston, the nearest town that would have a store selling really nice belt buckles. It was only seven miles away on a busy highway. Lowell and I had taken the train—Boston to Chicago to Livingston, Montana. We were dependent on Bill's auto and truck, as well as his skills at guiding hunters and being a strong rancher. I did not want to tie up either of Bill's vehicles just to go into Livingston for a fancy buckle for a girl. During the war, I had become used to hitchhiking, and when in uniform, rides were easy and many.

It was October. At night it could be quite cold in that mountain country. I had just helped put our horses away and had on my riding boots with the two-inch heels. It was late afternoon and soon would be dark. I told Lowell that I was going to hitch a ride and head for town. His comment still rings in my memory: "Have fun." I planned to.

I must have already been in love with Mildred, as I was so blank about what I was now doing. Memories have a way of changing a little over long periods, and as I began writing this story, I couldn't believe my memory of what had happened. I wrote to that little girl Mary Lynn in 2015. We have been friends for sixty-eight years. I asked her if it really was thirteen miles from her dad's ranch to Livingston and back to the ranch. Her answer was yes.

I walked from the ranch house to the highway, about three hundred feet, and walked toward town. There were quite a few autos and truckers heading for town, and so was I. It was now dark. No offers of a ride from anyone. I could not walk very fast with those two-inch heels, but I finally made it into town to the buckle store and made my purchase. It was now almost nine o'clock.

The ranch was seven miles away. I was very aware of my two-inch heels, and I was cold. There were no taxis available. Back then, it was a cash world, and I had no money. I had just spent all of my money on a buckle. There was one choice. Try for a ride back toward the ranch, and if there were no offers, walk the seven miles again. It was the loneliest three hours I can remember. There were no lights at all on that highway except when one of the very few cars went speeding by. The sky was totally black. I arrived at the ranch just about midnight. The next day I learned that hitchhiking had been banned because of an unsolved murder. It pays to ask many questions before you try something that could be close to stupidity.

GREAT HORNED OWL

69

A great horned owl is a magnificent example of a bird of prey. It is a night hunter. When you look into the eyes of one of these birds, you can imagine its ability to see in the dark, to leave its roost on silent wings, to weave through the forest at amazing speed, and to catch its target in steel-like talons.

I was eager to have one of these birds for a trophy. My chance came one wet and cold October day in 1947. I was on a big-game hunting trip in Montana, with photographs as my primary mission. Finding I had a few extra days, I managed to do some trophy hunting on my own. Deep in the forest, I heard its call, and I felt the hairs on the back of my neck tingle. I moved slowly and carefully toward the sound. The sound came again, and a few minutes later I was able to see my trophy high in a tree, about two hundred feet away.

I aimed my rifle and fired, and down came one of the largest great horned owls I had ever seen. Its wingspan from tip to tip was over five feet. Its talons were larger than my hands, with grasping needle-sharp claws. Its curved beak was nearly three inches long, and with its needle-sharp, pointed upper beak, it could tear almost anything to pieces.

As I approached, I stopped short. I was looking at a creature whose only interest left in its life was to tear me into tiny bits. I was looking at raw rage. I hope that I never see such evil again. It has never left me. If the wounded bird could have attacked me, it would have totally destroyed me. My bullet had passed through the chest of the bird, leaving a round hole the size of a silver dollar. The bird should have died instantly, but great horned owls have great strength and stamina. It was serving this bird well. Soon, its life was gone, and that dying owl ended any desire for trophies I ever had. Since I shot that owl, my desire to hunt any living creature has diminished and is almost gone entirely. A camera is my weapon now.

THE SHOOTING BLUNDER

70

In Big Game Country, every guide I have known in the field has had his rifle with him or within easy reach at all times. When an amateur hunter from any peopled location enters the guide's world of big-game animals, it becomes the guide's responsibility to keep the hunter out of harm's way.

Dick Randall worked as a guide in big bear country in Montana. I remember his telling me about the hunter who wounded a grizzly. The bear charged the hunter. Under those conditions, the hunter's backup is the guide. The grizzly is extremely fast and, when upset, a fearsome killing machine. Seconds count, and you have no time to run. You need to be a good shot, have great courage, and be very religious.

The hunter that Dick was telling me about was in imminent danger of a frightful death. He was saved by the quick ability and judgment of his guide, who was able to kill the bear that dropped just six feet from the hunter.

I decided to hunt alongside the Yellowstone River. I was able to shoot a very large black bird, but it fell into the river and began to float away. I really wanted that bird. I put my rifle down and followed the floating bird along the riverbank.

I spotted a tree that had fallen into the river, with its roots still anchored in the ground, and it looked like the bird would float close to it. Cowboy boots were not designed for this sort of thing, but I climbed out on to that downed tree. I was able to get out over the river about fifteen feet. It was cold in mid-October, and it was time to wear layers of clothing to keep warm.

The bird came toward me, and I was ready. There it was, just five or six feet away. I leaned far out and caught hold of the bird's neck, just as the last root holding the tree in place gave up. With my weight on the tree trunk and leaning way out like I was doing, the tree simply rolled over. It was now on top of me, and I was over my head in ice-cold river water, but I held on to that bird.

With teeth chattering, I made it to shore with my prize. I searched for my rifle, found it, and located my horse, which shied away when it saw a dripping rider carrying a huge black creature, also soaking wet.

Together, we finally made it back to the ranch house. I was frozen. Bill Randall's wife, Helen, seemed to be used to minor incidents like this. She pulled out her giant metal washtub and said, "You need a hot bath." The tub was large enough for a man to sit in if he had his knees up under his chin. Helen began filling the tub with hot water. I considered Helen and little Mary Lynn, so wearing my wet white underpants, I climbed in and sat down.

Lowell Wentworth had used the same tub. I still blame myself for not taking his picture. The only place with room for the tub was the kitchen. In that tiny house, the kitchen was the busiest room. Some experiences are never forgotten.

The next day, Bill Randall drove me into Livingston to visit the taxidermist. I took my prize with its six-foot wingspan and put it on the counter. The taxidermist took one look at it and roared, "Get that damned bald eagle the hell out of my shop! If I am caught with it, I face a $500 fine. And if you get caught with it, you will have to pay a $500 fine for killing it."

It seems that it was a young bald eagle, before it was old enough to have the white feathers.

So much for my trophy with all its agonies. We had a nice burial.

Mary Lynn in the washtub

OUR ALASKAN HIGHWAY ADVENTURE

71

Bob Dow and George plan the trip

Robert Dow, usually known as Bob, became interested in my plan to buy a four door French midget gasoline operated automobile which had just arrived in the US. Glenn Whitham, a long time family friend was an auto dealer in Boston MA. Glenn agreed to help with my plan. Bob was intrigued and we got together to plan it.

It proved to be a very tough project. We worked on the plan for nearly a year. Bob really joined me on every decision we had to make. I am sure the project would have failed without Bob. We became good friends and remain friends to this day.

I do not remember a single argument in the three months of driving together. He never appeared upset even when we had car troubles, lodging problems, road problems (of which there were many) or whatever came up. We agreed to be partners during this awesome trip, and thanks to Bob we made it.

The garage where we bought our little rear-engine Renault was a sponsor, of sorts, of our Alaskan adventure. At the time, we felt we could not make public some of the problems that we encountered with the car. There was certainly no mention in the newspapers. Now, over sixty years have gone by, so maybe the time has come.

Bob and I finally made it to Edmonton, Alberta, Canada. From Boston, it is a pretty long trip in itself. We had been on the *Welcome, Traveler* show in Chicago, and now we were in the capital of the Canadian province of Alberta. We had a chance to find a place to stay that we could afford that also offered a chance to freshen up. We were still pressed for time. Our travels were just beginning to make us realize how huge our planned trip actually was.

We stopped to have lunch in a nice Chinese restaurant. There seemed to be questions that required answers everywhere we went. The tiny rear-engine Renault was attracting interest everywhere we drove, and Edmonton was no exception. An interesting bit of information came to light. Canada did not allow dishtowels in any restaurants. All washed dishes had to air-dry. Canadian authorities believed that dishtowels could be dirty, spread germs, and generally be bad news.

Over lunch, we talked about our trip with a very nice Chinese gentleman who, as it turned out, owned the restaurant. When we were ready to leave, our new friend gave us a basket full of canned Chinese food to take with us. "Just in case you have trouble along the way," he said.

We did enjoy the food. From Edmonton to the start of the Alcan began our introduction to difficult road conditions. My memory tells me it was still around three hundred miles to mile number one in Dawson Creek. We found that dirt roads were more and more common.

The Renault was not designed for the five thousand miles of dirt and gravel roads that we subjected it to. For instance, we were using two-ply tires, and the recommendation at the time was six-ply. We went through seven tires in addition to the four new tires we were riding on—a total of eleven tires for the complete trip. That had nothing to do, however, with what happened that day, Monday, September 19, 1949.

We were on our way back down the Alaskan Highway, about seventeen miles below Summit Lake. Bill was driving when the car suddenly came to a stop. We got out to see what had happened. The first thing we noticed was that the back wheels were splayed. The bottoms were out and the tops were in, and the engine was sitting on the road. (No pictures, please!)

We were on a curve cut from a hill. The land went up quite steeply on one side of the road and just as steeply down the other side. There was no place for us to camp. In fact, the situation looked so hopeless that we just stood there and laughed. How were we going to get out of this one? We ate some sardines and cooked a little on the camp stove as it began to get chilly. Finally, about eight thirty in the evening, a truck came along, and we hitched a ride back to Summit Lake, where we booked a motel room for the night.

A fellow named Bert Palmer, a mechanic from the road commission service area for the trucks and equipment that maintained the highway, had seen our car when we passed through on our way to Alaska, and he recognized it. He took a look at our disaster and reported that it was not as serious as it seemed. He thought he could fix it but on his own time. He was not supposed to work on private vehicles. Bert told us he would pick up our car the next time he had a truck with him that could handle it. In the meantime, we stayed at the hotel and played cribbage in the lobby while we waited.

We did visit the Repeater Station, a telegraph-relay building nearby that kept information flowing up and down the highway (and enabled us to wire for money). It was run by the Gallants, a nice young couple that we met on the way up. They invited us to dinner, and then we went to the service area to see a movie called *Lifeboat*. While we waited for the car to be rescued, we explored the area with Ed Gallant, climbed the hills, and took lots of pictures.

Bert finally retrieved the Renault, and over the next few days, he got it running again. Total charge: ten dollars! On Monday, September 26, we were finally back on the road again, headed home.

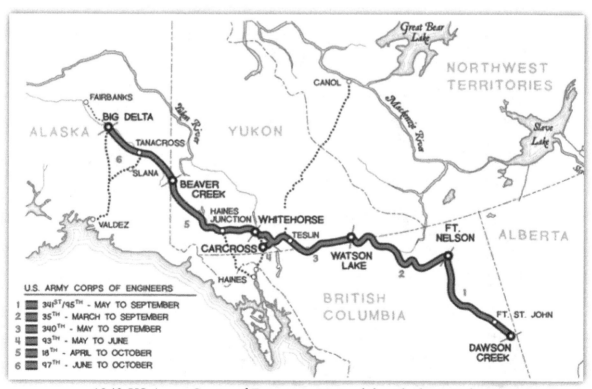

1942 US Army Corps of Engineers Map of the Alaskan Highway

The Renault packed and ready to go

ROAD TEST
FRENCH RENAULT
BOSTON TO
ALASKA AND
BACK
3 MONTHS
15000 MILES
5000 DIRT MI.
WEIGHT EMPTY
1200 lbs.
WEIGHT LOADED
2412 lbs.
2 PERSON CREW
11 TIRES, 2 PLY
268 SPARE PARTS
3 BATTERIES
ENGINE REBUILT
TWICE IN FIELD
62 CHANGES
NEEDED
MAX TEMP
117 F
LOW TEMP
18 F

The gear inside and on top of the car

RENAULT 4CV – ALASKAN-ALCAN-HIGHWAY-BOSTON-FAIRBANKS-R/T
Trial Test Run   Model Year: 1949   Miles: 12269   Dates: 7/28 to 10/26/1949---91 days

Weight: Empty- 1200 lbs. Add: 64 spare parts, 3 standard 2 ply spare tires, 1 spare auto battery, needed maintenance travel items and clothing for the test run crew of 2 men during the heat of summer and the oncoming Arctic fall, one sealed emergency 3006 rifle required by the Canadian authorities, camping equip-ment capable of servicing two men for five days in case of emergency due to the type of travel expected and the difficult Canadian dirt roads that provide access to the ALCAN, only recently opened for tourists travel. The added weight of all this is 600 lbs. The additional added weight of the crew at 320 lbs brings the total weight on the test run to 2120 lbs. This requires the smallest 4 door sedan that is in normal manufacture anywhere in the world to carry 67% of its own weight through the entire test. The engine in this small automobile is in the rear, storage is in the front under the hood. The car is not air conditioned. A movable curtain is in front of the motor and can be raised and lowered to allow heat or cool air to enter the cabin. The driver and passenger have bucket seats in front and a single seat wide enough for two in back. It is a very tight rear compartment for adults but provides storage for a long trip. Between 35 and 45 miles per gallon is expected but remains a question until the end of this test run due to the very heavy load being carried.

The specifics

Everything is impossible until someone does it!

TOMMY BARTLETT'S "WELCOME TRAVELERS"

N B C broadcast sponsored by Dreft, Drene and Spic and Span, originates Monday through Friday in the world-famous COLLEGE INN, HOTEL SHERMAN, CHICAGO; 9:00 to 9:30 A.M., Chicago time. Tommy plays host—in the COLLEGE INN—to approximately 3500 travelers weekly from every state in the Union and from all over the world. Every day millions of people tune in the "WELCOME TRAVELERS" radio show.

(L to R: Bob Cunningham, Jim Ameche, Tommy Bartlett, Les Lear)

Tommy Bartlett speaks about Bob and George's
Alaskan Journey before it begins

To this tiny Renault weighing 1200 pounds, George Perkins and Robert Dow added an additional 1000 pounds —themselves and their equipment.

Welcome Travelers, which originates in the College Inn of Chicago's Hotel Sherman, is broadcast Mon.-Fri. at 10 A.M. over NBC.

Tommy Bartlett sits next to the open door with Bob
behind him and George in the back seat

Mile one marker Alcan Highway

The actual road surface

The highway

Renault and 18 Wheeler Side by Side

Renault and Horse Side by Side

Our Melrose, Massachusetts screening

Our advertisement for the screening

MIDGET CAR VANQUISHES ALASKA ROAD

TWO-WAY JAUNT up Alaska Highway and back in tiny French Renault car was accomplishment of Robert Dow, left, and George Perkins, two Boston, Mass., university students. Equipped with sleeping bags, gas stove and food, pair covered 5,500 miles without mishap. Renault is first car of its kind to reach Fairbanks famed High-way.

TOPSIDE

72

Bob Dow and I were taking pictures in Alaska in August 1949. We noticed another man with his motion picture camera on a heavy tripod. I recognized him; it was Ted Phillips. I had great respect for Ted. He was an excellent producer and travel photographer, and I knew he did work for Burton Holmes. We stopped and talked with him for a short time. He told us that he was producing an Alaskan travelogue for Holmes's 1950 season. This meant that I would be able to see the finished product at Symphony Hall in Boston in January 1950.

This chance meeting, which lasted less than a half hour, changed my entire future. I believe it was a simple occurrence, entirely by chance, but it was caused by our being friendly and inquisitive. This suggests the importance of always having an open mind and giving time and thought to everything around us so that the time we have can give the greatest pleasure and opportunity to us.

Bob and I finished our Alaskan adventure and returned to Boston. Just by chance, I read in the newspaper that Ted Phillips was sick. I had never met Burton Holmes, but my own experience suggested he might be in trouble with Ted's Alaskan film because it had to be edited and the narration prepared. I was sure that the first showing of the film to the public was close at hand, and I wondered how detailed Ted's notes on Alaska might be. Bob and I had just spent close to three months on our trip, covering most of the same territory, and thanks to Bob's detailed notes, I thought perhaps I could be of help.

Holmes's home address was "Topside" in Hollywood. I knew that he also had a home in New York City that he used when he had shows in the East. I was able to obtain his telephone number and called him. He answered the call. Hearing that remarkable voice speaking to me directly, after having listened to his narrations for over ten years at Symphony Hall, I almost lost it. I said hello.

As it turned out, Mr. Holmes was in trouble. We actually became friends on that telephone call. I left for New York the next day. He arranged for parking close to his apartment. The doorman was expecting me. The elevator worked. Burton Holmes opened his front door, and we shook hands.

The next two days went by far too quickly for me. I learned that all of his friends called him by his initials, BH. He was the world's greatest living traveler. He was welcome anywhere he decided to travel because he was also a gentleman. He had earned his place in the annals of great men. He was also a kind man, and had brought world travel to more people than any other person in history.

His narrations were always of a positive nature. He had married late in life, at about age forty-six. His wife, Margaret, had difficulty hearing. She commented to me that it was beneficial at times.

At the end of the two-year time period in which each Holmes film is the busiest, BH gave the Alaska film to me. I still have it, and if all goes well, I plan to have it converted to gold disk. It may be the only Burton Holmes Travelogue in the world that is not in the preservation museum of the University of Southern California. I am sure this is not important to anyone else, but it means a great deal to me.

SUCCESS IS A WORD

73

Success is a word that means many different things. It is a wonderful word, but I do not enjoy its use because it's so broadly referred to. It is much easier for me to use the word *successful* because it can be focused on a single subject.

I have never felt that I am a success, but I do feel that I have been successful. To me being successful means being happy with my life. As I've mentioned, my father was fifty-one when I was born, and my mother was thirty-seven. Dad was a wise and happy man. I remember what he told me the day I turned sixteen:

"Son, I want you to listen to me very carefully. You have a choice to make, and it needs to be understood. You do not have to die to go to heaven or to go to hell. It is your choice from now on. You have the power to enjoy a bit of heaven while you are alive. You can also make the decision to create your own heaven or hell before you die. It is your choice. You will have many opportunities to make your choices. Think about me when you are faced with them."

On that day my father gave me the right to be the happy person I am. Great and kind people have helped me with those decisions all of my life. When I was thirteen, my grandfather told me the beavers had dammed the ranch irrigation ditch. He sent me up to the creek where the beaver dam was huge. It was about twenty feet wide and six feet thick and so carefully woven that I could not move much of it. I worked on it for hours. The next morning, Gramp said the water was still backed up. He said, "Come with me."

He took a little stick with him. We walked to the dam. He looked at me and said, "Grandson, I am going to teach you how to think when you are working. When you have a job to do, think about it, and study it to find the easiest and quickest way to complete it." With that, he pushed the little stick carefully into the beaver dam, lit its fuse, and the dynamite let the water through. To this day, I consider each job I have carefully.

Great wealth has never been a part of my plan. I needed to travel. I needed to be known as a professional. I needed friends on whom I could rely to tell me the truth when I was off base. I needed to be known for my honesty, truthfulness, quality, thoughtfulness, and—above all—my independence. I had learned early in life that the giver is always happier than the receiver. It has always been true. My friends have always been available to me for counsel. They have shown me that life can and should be fun. Every day can bring a surprise, and every day can also bring difficulties.

I have never feared failure. Failure gives birth to new and better ideas. It's important to know that you are still trying every time you look in the mirror. Challenge is a wonderful aphrodisiac. Constant trying makes life fun. Make a game out of life, and you will have won.

I have filled my life with enjoyable memories, and I think of them every day. When things go wrong or fail to work out, my dearest friend taught me to let them go. Do not waste time with them. Only think of them for a moment to be sure you don't make the same mistake again. Concentrate on your future.

Most of all, laugh at yourself often, and if you have really blown it, laugh harder. It makes a great impression on people, and it's very good for your mental health. I think I am about to laugh.

BURTON HOLMES, THE GREATEST TRAVELER

74

When I was twenty-four, the most famous traveler in the world was Burton Holmes. He was a seasoned traveler and advised visitors to bring letters of introduction to "people of wealth or position" if the newcomers wanted to enjoy a luau in a private Honolulu house in Waikiki, a charming suburb about three miles from the center of Honolulu.

On the other hand, monarchs were often honored guests at social events given by *haole* (Caucasians) who lived in Waikiki. At one party he attended, Holmes said the host and hostess met him with a lei before he could reach the house. Quaint Japanese maids in native costume brought them appetizers, and then he went to the lanai, where the luau was spread. Ferns were laid on the floor, and stacked in the center and spilling out to the edges were pineapple, watermelon, other fruits, and sometimes a stalk of sugar cane. Everything was placed on the table at once: pink crabs, baby lobsters, baked mullet in ti leaves (and unwrapped by the hostess, who broke it and passed around pieces to guests). The highest compliment was to "suck one's fingers as audibly as possible" and withdraw the fingers from the mouth with a satisfied smack in appreciation of the cuisine.

Burton Holmes was the first man to bring a portable motion picture camera into both Russia and Japan. Every year he produced and presented five new motion pictures of the world to the public in the greatest auditoriums in the United States, including Symphony Hall in Boston, Orchestra Hall in Chicago, and Carnegie Hall in New York. He was truly a very great man and one of the finest men I have ever known.

I was with him when he appeared at Carnegie Hall. We took the heavy case holding the motion picture that he would present that evening from his home to the hall in a taxi. He always arrived an hour early. When we arrived at Carnegie, we went to his dressing room. He was one of America's best-dressed men. He always appeared on stage in white tie and tails. Every seat in the great hall was sold. He said to me, "Please take the film up to the projection booth." That was when I realized that the film was still in the taxi and long gone. I was in absolute shock. In just forty-five minutes, every seat in the grand hall would be filled with paying customers.

At that moment, Mr. Holmes taught me one of the most important lessons in my life. Holmes continued to dress. He said, "This is a situation we cannot control. I must finish my dressing because I may have to tell the audience our film has been lost. I want you to relax. Just sit down and think of the situation so it will never happen again."

He was not angry with me at all. We had both forgotten to bring the film. Fifteen minutes before curtain time, the cab driver who had driven us arrived with the film. His next passenger had found the case in the back seat of the cab, and the driver knew it had to belong to Holmes. I remember that day every time I am faced with an insurmountable problem. If you cannot control it, relax, have patience, and think.

Holmes also taught me to understand the word *competition*. He taught me to understand that a competitor is anyone to whom you can be compared. He also taught me that the way I looked would set the initial opinion of my value to a new or old customer. He also demanded that I wear a hat that was always there and always very visible. There were two major reasons for this: (1) it made it easy to locate me in a hurry, and (2) it made it easy to start a conversation. It works.

"SHE SAID YES!"

75

Mildred and I were engaged to be married. Finally, after three refusals and a *no* from her father, she relented and said yes. But even then, the word *wait* was in her vocabulary. Plans for our wedding began in earnest.

A dinner dance was held in the Melrose Memorial Hall just a few days after Mildred agreed to be my wife. It had been a long four-year effort to reach that point. I was overwhelmingly happy to have won this most important effort in my life. My friends were there, and I needed to tell them the great news. However, I almost blew it all. I went to introduce her, and I could not come up with her name. This has not been forgotten.

My wife, Mildred

LESSON ONE BY BABY GEORGE, THE TEACHER

76

Our master bedroom in our apartment had a good-sized dressing area that was perfect when our first baby, George, came home from the hospital with his mother. He had a wonderful head of black hair that was so thick and long the nurses referred to him as "Porcupine."

He was my first experience with a baby, and being a father was a brand new and unnerving situation for me. The day Mildred, carrying little George, walked into our apartment, I learned just how fortunate I had become. My dear wife was the oldest girl and the second oldest child in her family of father, mother, and four sons and three daughters. To add to my astonishment, I began to appreciate her mother, who believed in everyone having their jobs to do. Etta was a remarkable mother-in-law to me.

She was a woman who had relied on her oldest daughter to do just about everything. She taught her to cook, clean, handle laundry, and do everything a new mother, with a totally unprepared and untrained new father, suddenly had to know how and what to do.

The learning that a new father has to accept can have almost awesome overtones. Take diapers, for instance. If they are new and clean, they are quite okay, but then the baby wears them, and that changes everything. Mildred told me that I was doing very well.

Little George was gaining weight and length. He was, in fact, a real handful. The day came when he decided to take my training into his own little hands. He needed to be changed and was an expert at letting me know. I took him into his area off the master bedroom and put him up on the changing table. I opened his diaper and was surprised that it really wasn't that bad. Lesson one by baby, the teacher. He waited for just the right moment and proved he was a baby boy by hitting me in the face, including my nose and both eyes. It was very warm.

Once dried off, I knew I needed to put a dry diaper on the little one. I took hold of his two ankles and lifted his bottom up off the changing table to slide the diaper under him. At that moment, he told me why he had been fussing in the first place. He released a large amount of pressure caused by the storage of gas. When it blew, it ruined the wallpaper at the end of the room at least *eight* feet away. Education can really take hard turns at times.

NIAGARA TO NEWFOUNDLAND

77

In 1952, Lowell and I filmed *Niagara to Newfoundland*. It was a big order. We started at Niagara Falls on the Canadian side. Toronto was next, with its huge annual fair. Then we went north to the Chateau Laurier in Canada's capital city of Ottawa. Lowell moved into the national park to film beavers. I had a good deal of help from Pieret Seguin, who worked at the radio station in the hotel. She helped me see the unique side of this famous city. Karsh, perhaps the most famous portrait photographer in the world, had his studio there. I dreamed about sitting for a personal portrait with him, but neither my time nor my budget allowed it.

Lowell, with his wife, Alice, moved on to Quebec to film the Saint Lawrence River and Seaway. The haze was so severe they were "forced" to stay many days and nights in the great Chateau Frontenac, one of the Canadian Pacific hotels. We were lucky that the railroad executives allowed us to use the hotel without cost because of our ability to bring its story to the American public. Sadly, the haze finally lifted, and the filming resumed.

By this time, Mildred had given birth to our first son on June 29. We named the little one George William Perkins III. It seemed like such a large name for a tiny baby. It was another moment in my life when my dear wife proved to be adventurous and remarkable. I truly knew how strong she was, but she kept proving it, just to be sure.

I had to film Newfoundland, and it could not wait any longer due to a booking deadline. I had delayed leaving until she gave birth, but now I had to leave. Mildred had two choices: She could stay at home with our newborn son, or she could bring a two- to three-week-old baby on a very difficult trip. The trip entailed the following:

o Driving one thousand miles
o Leaving the car and taking the overnight ferry from Sydney to Port aux Basques

o Taking the narrow-gauge railroad across the great island, a twenty-six-hour ride, sitting up
o Constantly caring for a tiny baby
o Nursing and changing our very active baby in about every type of location you could think of, with little or no privacy:
    ▪ In the auto
    ▪ On the ferry
    ▪ On the train
    ▪ In the restaurant
    ▪ In the hotels
    ▪ On the plane
    ▪ In the wild hunting and fishing areas with no electricity

Yes, of course she decided to go with me! What the heck? The baby could handle it, and she could handle it. But could I handle it?

I now know that babies are amazingly strong and resilient. In this day and age, they are catered to in unnecessary ways, but I would not change a thing. I also know how strong and steadfast a supportive woman can be when the man she loves needs her.

We carried four suitcases. Three of them were full of disposable diapers because at that time, they were not available where we were working. The other suitcase had the clothing for the baby, for me, and—wonder of wonders—for Mildred. We have been back several times since that hard first trip, and we find our memories are indeed precious.

There were two weeks of heavy filming in the Bowaters paper mill at Cornerbrook, where trees were made into newsprint. We had to walk down the steep, wet, slippery clay cliffs to the Humber River below to film the salmon jumping the Humber Falls. Mildred had to carry our son while I carried the tripods, cameras, and necessary production equipment. We then had to walk the shoreline and climb the rocky coast, being careful not to fall when the huge Newfoundland dogs showed they were glad to see us. We also had to load and unload the rented auto dozens of times, and at the very end, there was the fifty-mile nighttime dash over a dirt road in a jeep as we tried not to miss the ferry on the way home, but we did it. Filming is hard work, and it takes deep concentration.

Our first trip to Newfoundland

ALONE WITH HIROSHI, A TOKYO PROFESSOR

78

In 1979, I was staying alone in the Miyako Hotel in San Francisco. At breakfast I noticed a pleasant, rather slender, professional-appearing man eating alone. I remember smiling at him, and a brief smile was returned. During the morning, we passed each other several times in the lobby and nodded pleasantly to each other.

Lunchtime came, and we both entered the dining room at the same time. We both were still alone, so I said, "Why not sit together? I am from Boston, and I prefer the Japanese Miyako over the other hotels in this city."

The man said, "My name is Hiroshi Ikari. I am a professor in Tokyo. I am alone and having lunch with you will be very pleasant."

At that moment I knew we were destined to be close personal friends. The old chemistry was working again, just as it had worked for me so many times before. We humans should remember that we tend to reap what we sow.

From that day until Hiroshi's death over thirty years later, our friendship remained strong. Hiroshi was a professor of American history. He brought many Japanese college students to Boston, and several even visited our home. In the heat of summer, they enjoyed our swimming pool. It is clean, clear, circulating, and delightful. The Japanese take great pleasure in bathing. We were surprised that the college students wanted to take a shower and bathe as soon as they finished swimming. Several of those students have stayed in touch at least once a year since those days in the 1980s and early '90s.

Hiro and Tomiko, his delightful wife, visited us about fifteen years ago. We had visited them in 1989, during our "around the world flight." Tomiko and one of Hiro's students and friends paid us a brief visit. I remember when our sons were relatively young, and Hiro sat in our living room talking about World War II. He amazed us when he explained that the end of the war was brought to a quick close by the terrible atom bombs that destroyed Hiroshima and Nagasaki. Hiro's family was from Hiroshima, and many were lost there.

Hiro told us that the war would have dragged on for perhaps a dozen years because the Japanese would have refused to yield due to their beliefs. Thousands more Japanese and Americans would have died. It could have destroyed Japan. As a part of the surrender, General MacArthur preserved the position of the emperor. The warlords who chose the war were not able to force a continuation of the war in the face of such awesome damage to Japan as Hiroshima and Nagasaki and with the protected position of the emperor in the surrender terms.

I showed Hiro some of our old and cherished landmarks and buildings that in some cases went back over three hundred years. Hiro was very respectful of them. As he was about to leave for home, he suggested that I visit him in Tokyo. While there, he said he would show me some of the Japanese buildings that were five thousand years old. In 1989 we did visit Hiroshi and Tomiko in Tokyo, and we did see some of their truly ancient monuments.

I have tried to put all my valued memories of these dear friends together. I believe they were able to visit us five times to our one journey to see them. Our Japanese visiting "daughter", Mayumi Kitaoka, is now a dear friend thanks to her introduction to us by Hiroshi and Tomiko.

WRONG BOARDING PASSES

79

Today is November 17, 2001, a Saturday. Mildred and I are on our way home from a seven-day conference at the Atlantis Resort in the Bahamas. We arrived at the airport in plenty of time to make Mildred happy, although I don't think there is any "sport" in being early. It is when you are late that the excitement becomes intense! However, we were sitting in the waiting room, and Mildred was studying our boarding passes. She discovered that our luggage had been shipped to Miami, not Boston, and we had someone else's tickets. This meant we might miss a very tight connection and the only available plane from Atlanta to Boston to fly on that day.

Mil took off with her hand trunk and two jackets, pulling her wheeled carry-on with her laptop computer inside, weighing approximately forty pounds. Our gate was a long way away, and she was really moving. We were told the plane was boarding. I was following, dragging my own wheeled carry-on and panting and perspiring. We made it to the plane, which was very crowded. She was alone in her seat; I was on the other side of the plane, six seats away. Mildred attempted to lift her carry-on into the overhead bin; no one offered any help. She got her dander up and shoved and pushed, and by gosh, she got it into the overhead storage, which was easily eighteen inches above her head.

She turned around and, with a devastatingly engaging smile, spoke to the world, declaring, *"I did it!"* Why do I love this character, this woman, this incredible seventy-three-year-old grandmother? If I had time, I could count a couple of thousand different reasons, but unbounded spirit is definitely one of them.

BURTON HOLMES AND JOHN STODDARD

80

This is a beautiful and challenging day. How fortunate for me to awaken and again know the ultimate joy in my life. My wife, Mildred, is still asleep beside me, allowing me the pleasures of awakening her for another day together.

Today, memories take me back to age twelve and watching the Burton Holmes Travelogues at Symphony Hall in Boston with my folks. As I've mentioned, travel was one of my dad's greatest joys. He looked forward to showing me how much enjoyment it would give me when I learned about the whole world firsthand.

Burton Holmes was unique among the men and women who brought travel to the public. On stage in white tie and tails and wearing the speaker's white gardenia in his lapel, Holmes made his stories about his motion pictures—in all their beautiful colors and excitement—a truly living experience.

By the end of the nineteenth century, John L. Stoddard of Boston, Massachusetts, was the greatest travel lecturer in the world. Travel was still an adventure. His death in June 1931 followed a thirty-four-year absence from appearing in public due to his failing health. Any person fortunate enough to have enjoyed him at his best was privileged indeed. His vivid descriptions, natural eloquence, sonorous voice, and dominant personality made an abiding impression of greatness.

A few years before this highly educated, renowned traveler left the presenter's podium, he met a young travel photographer in Chicago named Burton Holmes. Holmes told me that John invited him to visit Oberammergau, Germany, and spend a few days with John. At that point, John was beginning to feel his age but not admitting to it.

Burton Holmes began his own photo presentations in the Chicago area. He told me when we first met that his love of travel created his much-used comment, "To travel is to possess the world." Note please, possess is not own – how wise he was.

DEATH VALLEY AND ITS PERILS

81

In the summer of 1939, while we were in California, my dad decided to visit Death Valley. It was about nine hours by car from Los Angeles, and there were no main highways. We had to climb over the Panamint Mountains and down the other side to actually enter the Valley. We stopped in Panamint Springs and visited the daughter of William Cody, known as Buffalo Bill. Miss Cody advised us not to try to cross the desert in the daytime. Cars had no air conditioning back then, and they could boil over in the 120-plus temperatures. It was late July, and no one who knew Death Valley drove across it at high noon, but my dad was used to the heat of Panama and wasn't worried. She gave us water to take with us, and off we went.

If you drive to Death Valley, you can still see wild donkeys along the highway. They are descended from the animals that lived there in the prospecting days. Their ancestors came with the miners and prospectors. We stopped to feed them on our trip and found some to be friendly and others aloof or skittish. We were very careful around them, as they can give a painful bite and a wicked kick. We enjoyed the experience, and then continued on our way.

When we arrived at the bottom of the Valley, we were 220 feet below sea level. Halfway across the Valley, we heard the sharp sound of breaking glass. We had a little glass thermometer inside the car. The temperature had reached 130 degrees, and the thermometer burst!

The wind coming into the automobile was so hot it seemed to be scorching us. Mother kept wetting handkerchiefs and putting them on our faces. Sure enough, after the thermometer burst, the engine overheated and boiled over. Dad stopped and added some of the water Miss Cody had given us, and we finally reached the only place in the Valley that had water. It was called Furnace Creek, a fitting name.

We bought gas, ice water, and cold drinks. There was an old desert-dweller sitting in the shade, and Dad offered him a drink of water.

"Water?" he said.

Dad said, "Yes."

"I haven't been used to drinking water in years," he said, but he accepted. As he was about to take a sip, he said, "Over the teeth and over the gums, look out stomach; here it comes!" Then he thought for a minute and said, "Here's to ya and toward ya. If I hadn't seen ya, I wouldn't have knowed ya!" Then he drank the strange fluid called water.

I have been told that it is so hot in Death Valley that a rattlesnake could die of exposure in fifteen minutes if it can't get out of the sun at high noon. Scorpions and other desert creatures play, hunt, and eat at night. We didn't see much wildlife in the hot daytime hours.

If you had a flat tire while driving across the Valley in the summertime, you could die from the heat while changing the tire if you didn't change it quickly. In 1939 tires were not the same quality or strength they are today. Driving across the desert at that time of year was not the smartest thing to do. Even the wonderful Furnace Creek Inn closes during the high summer season.

LIGHTWEIGHT CAMERA

82

The greatest traveler in the United States, Burton Holmes—BH, as his close friends called him—lived in Hollywood, with a second home in New York City. As a young man, he fell in love with the country of Japan and its people. He found great pleasure in the Buddhist religion.

He was a leader of the Camera Club in his hometown of Chicago and explained his love of travel and the scenes that he had photographed with his own narration. He was the first person to use the word *travelogue*, and it became instantly popular. He decided to take his travel pictures and his lectures to London. He was successful in the United States, but in London, no one would come because he charged a fee. He learned that in London, lectures were usually free.

Mr. Holmes had shown his photographs projected on a large screen. First, they were in black and white, and then he had artists in Japan add color to the individual glass slides by hand-painting them. After that, moving pictures in black and white arrived.

The Santa Fe Railroad asked him to make the first travel movies ever made for the first black-and-white television. Then, of course, motion pictures in color arrived. My dad and I loved the travelogues.

The first series that I remember included the coronation of Emperor Haile Selassie of Ethiopia, the oldest Christian country. Holmes was an honored guest. At the last moment, the parade route was changed. News photographers were using large heavy cameras. Holmes was the only person with a totally portable camera that allowed him to run quickly where needed. He shared the parade movies he took with the news people. The emperor was so pleased he awarded a special medal to Holmes for special service to his country.

In 1954, Mildred, our two-year-old son, George, and I attended a visit by the emperor to Athens, Greece. Memories of his coronation and knowing the details of the Holmes experience gave added excitement to our visit.

HOLMES, THE MAN

83

It was early in January 1950 that Burton Holmes wrote to his manager, Walter Everest, and told him that he had found an associate narrator for his world-famous travelogue series. I was that narrator. I had been to see his five new films shown at Symphony Hall in Boston each year since I was about twelve years old. I had only missed a few during the time I was in the navy and during World War II. At the age of twenty-four, I was about to be offered an opportunity that dreams are made of.

In our family, Burton Holmes had been in our conversations many times. He was the perfect example for my dad to enjoy because my dad loved to travel so much. Burton was also a prime example for a young man like me because he was one of America's best-dressed men. His reputation was classically revered. Lowell Thomas, the much honored and believed news commentator, wrote that Holmes was the finest man he had ever known.

BH was the first person to take a motion picture camera into Russia, and he was also the first person to take a motion picture camera into Japan. He did not marry until he was about forty-six, when he chose to marry a lovely lady. The first time I met her, I realized her ability to hear was a challenge. At that time, they had been married for over thirty years. BH was drawn to the Buddhist faith; Margaret was a Presbyterian. They had worked it all out. They went to her church to be married. Then, on the same day, they went to the Buddhist Church and were married again. It worked. They were in love.

When they arrived back at their apartment in New York City, BH realized they had enjoyed a very special day. He went back to the minister who had married them. BH noticed that the minister had worn a white wedding collar, BH asked if he could have it. Then he went to the Buddhist church and bought the five-foot-high statue of the Buddha they had stood before to be married.

*BH owned one of the great private collections of the Buddha,
over six hundred pieces. He then stood the Buddha statue in his
collection and placed the minister's white wedding collar around
the neck of the Buddha. I value my picture of that occasion.*

THE RHINE AT CARNEGIE HALL

84

I was contracted to present the travel motion picture *The Rhine* at Carnegie Hall in New York City. Andrew Carnegie was a great and remarkable man. He became enormously successful, but he never allowed his financial success to spoil his life. He limited his annual income and devoted much of his fortune to philanthropy.

He created Carnegie Hall. An enduring benefit that came to me by becoming a travelogue lecturer was the opportunity to stand alone on the grandest platforms of the greatest auditoriums in the United States, Canada, and Mexico. Once on the platform, I had the privilege of bringing the joys of seeing the world to my audiences.

There is a mystique about Carnegie Hall. Now I was at Carnegie alone. I was in the same dressing room I had been in with Holmes and the same dressing room that had been used by the greatest entertainers, politicians, and geniuses in all the world. Their ghosts seemed to still be there. I could see Holmes changing into his white tie and tails. I helped put his white gardenia in his buttonhole.

I settled in but made a side trip to check out the stage, then the projection booth, then the audience seating, and finally the ticket lobby that suddenly had come alive. The lines were forming as the people arrived. They had come to Carnegie Hall so I (and motion pictures) could take them to *The Rhine*. I came close to panicking, but being an "old-timer" in entertainment, I remembered the stage manager at the National Geographic Society in Washington, DC, when I lectured at Constitution Hall to a sold-out house on New England. The time came, and he said, "Okay, out you go, on your own or with a kick from me." That memory calmed me down.

At eight o'clock, the lights dimmed. I walked out onto that great stage alone. At the center I took my bow to the applause of the audience that filled the hall. I walked to my microphone and stood there for a moment, carefully committing to my memory the feelings that came over me as I studied every seat in the house. Then I began my show. Carnegie Hall was one of the most stimulating moments of my life.

The Burton Holmes Travelogues were always presented at Carnegie. One night, BH and I were on our way to Carnegie to present his new motion picture on Alaska, filmed by Ted Phillips, in honor of its statehood. We arrived, and I paid the taxi. Holmes and I entered the stage door, and Holmes said, "Please take the film to the projectionist." I said, "I do not have the film." We both realized the film had been left in the taxi. New York City has quite a few cabs.

At that moment I learned a very important lesson—very important! We had ninety minutes until show time and it was a sold-out house. Our film was driving around New York City in the back of a taxi, and we had no idea how to reach the driver. I looked in awe at Holmes. He stood there, kind of unconcerned. He said, "Let us go to our dressing room." I was in the process of totally freaking out.

Holmes put his hand on my arm. "I need to get dressed. There is nothing we can do about this. It is out of our control. There is no need to get excited. I just have to be ready to greet my audience and explain our problem. If you cannot control the situation, take a deep breath and make the best of it."

I was stunned. This man was at ease and was thinking ahead for what he would say to his sold-out audience. Twenty minutes of agony went by. I had been occupied with paying the taxi driver, but I still felt as if leaving the film in that taxi was my fault. Holmes did not blame me at all. Then Holmes got word that a taxi driver had just dropped off a motion picture at the Carnegie stage door. The driver said his next fare got in the back seat and asked him what was in the big heavy case. The driver said, "I looked at the case. I knew it was a film case. I knew my fare was at Carnegie. I knew it was a Holmes film there tonight. So I hurried over with it. Was I right?"

Could this really have happened to me in New York City with the greatest world traveler in the United States? Unbelievable, but it did.

NORTHERN ARTERY

85

The Faneuil Hall market area in Boston is a fun place to visit. It is usually quite crowded with new visitors, repeat visitors, and large numbers of people who work in Boston who come every chance they have.

At the age of eighteen and a senior in Melrose High School, I was lucky to have a job working for a wholesale beef seller who sold hips and tops primarily to restaurants and hotels. Harry Smith and my dad were longtime friends. During the summer of 1944, with high school behind me and Northeastern University to start in September, I had about three months to learn Harry's business. He knew the little secrets of making money in his world.

I weighed about 130 pounds, so Harry surprised me by telling me to deliver a 350-pound barrel of hips and tops to a restaurant on the second floor of the building where his business was located. To deliver that barrel, it was necessary to first roll it down the sidewalk about two hundred feet. I then had to stand it upright, call up to the restaurant on the second floor, and wait by the barrel so no one would steal it. Then I had to grab hold of the heavy rope that the chef dropped down, tie it around the barrel, making sure it would not slide off. It was a round barrel, and I had never handled a large rope or a round barrel before.

Once this delivery job was all set and the rope securely around the barrel, the roped barrel was lifted slowly up about twenty feet by a motor and dragged into the kitchen of the restaurant. I found my way back to Harry, who wanted to know why I had been gone so long.

Working for Harry Smith was a good education, provided it was for a short time. Harry and I lived in the same town of Melrose, Massachusetts. He planned to pick me up each morning and drop me off on his way home. One day he told me he was under the weather and asked me to do the driving. I had received my license over a year ago so that was no problem. On the way to Boston, the Northern Artery, as it was and still is known, was four lanes wide in one location. The road passed under a long bridge, and traffic was heavy.

As we neared the bridge, Harry's Cadillac suddenly started to skid. In fact, it started to do a complete circle at about thirty miles an hour. Something on the road had caused this—we never did learn what—but all I could do was hold on and hope. In all that traffic and at that speed, the circle was completed without contact with anything. The automobile straightened out and continued as if nothing had occurred. For the very first time, Harry was totally silent. He was also as white as a sheet.

A few days later, I borrowed a big old Harley-Davidson motorcycle from a friend. I had to be at work and did not have a ride that day. When I arrived at the market, the car in front of me stopped unexpectedly. I jammed on my brakes, tipping the motorcycle on its side as I lost my balance. I have been told that bike weighed about twelve hundred pounds. Once it was down, I couldn't lift it up. Traffic was unhappy. I had it all stopped while I fought to pick up the bike.

A very big African American who worked in the market strode out and, with the kindest words ("Oh, for C—— sake"), picked the bike up with one hand and walked out of the traffic and over to the curb. He handed the bike over to me and growled something like, "Grow up." It was one of my less-than-good days.

PEG IS MISSING

86

At nine o'clock at night, our doorbell rang. It was my close friend Dick Lawrence.

"I need your help," he said. "Peg is missing! She is suicidal, and her medication isn't helping. I'm afraid that if she takes another dose, it could kill her."

Dick had been dating Peg for some time and was really worried. I told my wife about Dick's problem and reached for my hat, jacket, and car keys. "Should I take my car?" I asked.

"Yes, we have to cover a wide range of locations quickly," Dick said. "I need you to check out every hotel and motel along Route 1 and Route 95 for about thirty miles, both north and south. Check the sign-in book in each place and look for the name of any single woman who arrived after six o'clock this evening. Peg might be using another name."

I worked as fast as I could. I understood his concerns and knew he was very involved with trying to help her. After about four hours, I had checked every place in the area without success. I knew Dick would work all night until he'd searched every single spot he could think of.

I knew one motel that Peg had used before and liked. I knew that would be his first stop. The next morning, he told me that had been his first and his last stop during the night, but no single woman had signed in. It bothered him until morning arrived. Then he went to check again, just to be sure.

There had been trouble at that motel. Apparently, the night clerk had pocketed the cost of the room and had not had her sign the register. When her room was opened for cleaning, Peg was found dead.

COWBOY COOK

87

The year 1939 became an amazing one for me at the age of thirteen. Bess Randall Erskine helped me learn to ride a horse, just like cowboys and cowgirls who controlled their horses and rode for hours at a time.

Dick Randall telling stories about his wife, Dora, and his children. Bess met her husband, Clyde Erskine, when he became an engineer. As it turned out, that was a huge help to Dick and Dora's future.

Building Dick's OTO Dude Ranch required an immense amount of hand labor, but there was a shortage of able workers. All of the buildings had to be built with fresh-cut logs and then dragged by horse and humans from the wilds of Montana to the ranch location. It required locating and sizing over one thousand trees.

Bess had married Clyde, who was in love with Bess and in love with the OTO ranch idea. He and Dick worked around the clock and succeeded in moving that large number of fresh-cut logs to the OTO location. Clyde was a happy surprise to Dick and Dora. He and Dick learned to cook remarkable meals over campfires when they took dudes hunting for weeks at a time.

Over the years, my time spent with both Bess and Clyde developed into a mutually appreciated friendship. Recently, I came across a happy remembrance of Clyde, who finally, years ago, retired to a warmer state with the first true retirement village known to me, Sun City, Arizona. *Better Homes and Gardens* had a cooking contest in June 1962. After cooking for all those wealthy hunters and tourists over the years at OTO, my dear friend Clyde won! Even now, my taste buds are reacting to his win.

Cookout recipe

Dude Ranch Beans

Pardner, these beans let you live those Westerns—

You'll need a large old-time cast-iron Dutch oven—at least 6-quart size—that has a lid with flange around it to hold hot coals and a handle in the center so a hook can be used to pick the lid up (see page 70). Dig a hole in the ground deep enough for the depth of your Dutch oven plus 3 inches of coals at top and bottom and 4 inches of earth over all; width of hole needs to be about 1½ times the diameter of your Dutch oven to allow for coals along the sides.*

- 2 pounds (about 4 cups) small navy beans
- ¼ teaspoon soda
- 1 teaspoon salt
- 1 teaspoon ginger
- 1 teaspoon dry mustard
- 2 tablespoons molasses
- 3 to 4 pounds uncooked ham

Soak beans overnight in 3 quarts cold water in Dutch oven. In the morning, add soda, cover, and bring just to boiling. Beans should be barely covered with liquid. Add seasonings and molasses; mix. Place ham in center of beans. Cover Dutch oven with preheated lid and lower onto 3-inch bed of hot coals in hole. Place more hot coals around Dutch oven and over lid to depth of 3 inches. Fill in the hole with about 4 inches of earth. Let cook 8 to 12 hours. Makes 12 to 15 servings.

Note: Erskine cooks a gallon of beans and a whole ham 12 to 14 hours. For a Dutch oven, 16 inches across, with 4 inches of coals at top and bottom plus 6 inches of dirt covering, he digs a hole 24 inches deep and 24 inches across.

*To cook indoors, using Dutch oven with kettle-type lid, bake in slow oven (300°) about 8 hours.

DAY ONE TO SEE ALL FORTY-EIGHT

88

Dad came home from work one night and said to Mother, "Daisy, I want to take you and our son into every single one of our United States, all forty-eight of them." Mother sat very still, and I can still remember the way she stared at Dad.

He said, "I never went to college, Daisy, but I worked on the canal in Panama and raised bananas in Costa Rica. I took people by train to the Grand Canyon, and all of this expanded my thinking. Travel is the greatest education there is for most of us. I want our son to know how to travel and how to learn from it."

Mother looked at Dad and studied his face for a long moment. Then she said, "You want to drive everywhere, don't you?" "Yes." Then Mother said softly, "When?"

"I have been accumulating my vacation time, and I have a new assistant who is doing well. Let's make the trip next summer. Bill will be thirteen."

Dad did not smoke or drink alcohol, and he drove in a carpool to work. Every time anyone smoked, he would put a nickel in his pocket as a way to save money. In two years, he saved enough for us to travel for almost two months.

Mother was still searching his face, and all she said was, "Next June?" Dad said, "Next July. Better for my office." She said, "Yes, we'll do it."

Dad put his hand on hers, and the rest of our dinner was quiet. I had no idea what next July would mean to me, but I would find out.

Late June 1939 arrived, and off we drove beginning our trip. That big old four-door, eight-cylinder 98 Oldsmobile was ready and packed with so much. I remember it well. Dad set me up in the back seat with plenty of room. Back then, there were no seat belts, almost no real highways, and gas was all leaded. The gas wars made pricing sometimes as low as ten cents a gallon. That automobile had a big gas tank and only got about ten miles per gallon.

Dad put all new tires on the car and hoped they would last the entire trip, which was estimated to be approximately seven thousand miles. There was no radio or air conditioning, and it was very hot. We knew nothing different and loved that old automobile.

THE DENNISONS

89

In 1940, when I was fourteen, I received a letter from William Dennison, the president of the Chelsea Savings Bank. It contained five unique pieces of United States paper money that Mr. Dennison had found in his desk at his office. He had saved them for many years and was glad to send them to me. He explained that before we had metal coins, as we do now, we used paper money to make change. In my letter, I enjoyed finding United States three-cent, five-cent, ten-cent, twenty-five-cent, and fifty-cent paper money dated 1810.

Bill Dennison and his wife, Myrtie, lived in Winchester, Massachusetts. I looked forward to visiting him at his bank all through my youth. He took his valuable time every time we visited to teach me a way of thinking about money that has been helpful. During the summers, my mother, dad and I visited Bill and his wife at their summer home in Gloucester quite often. Dad believed in lifetime friendships, and now, so do I.

In 1947, when I was twenty-one, Lowell Wentworth and I were photographing big-game hunting in Montana with the help of Bill Randall and Oliver Tenderlin, two very experienced ranchers and guides. Our mail from home in Melrose, Massachusetts, brought stories of wildfires in Maine and the other New England states. Several friends lost a large amount of property, and some were injured. We were sad indeed to learn that our dear friends the Dennisons lost their much-enjoyed summer home in Gloucester. I was impressed by the Dennisons' home when I found that they had a live-in apartment for their full-time maid on the third floor of their home. He was a kind and thoughtful man.

TWO TRAVELOGUE PIONEERS MEET

90

Long before I was born in 1926, Burton Holmes was rapidly gaining audiences eager to see more of his special worldwide photographs. While he was in London, he coined his word *travelogue*. Lowell Thomas commented, "Burton Holmes is the finest man I have ever known".

BH brought travel to more people than any other person during his nearly sixty years of standing on stages of the greatest auditoriums in the world. BH and Margaret, his wife, came to one of my very first travel lectures in 1949 in New York City. He asked me to join him, and I was overwhelmed. We were together for about fifteen years.

In 1954, I produced the very first wide-screen travelogue. BH and I came together in the field when this photograph and article appeared. It was an exceptional moment for me to be with such a great man in such a unique situation.

B-10 Los Angeles Herald & Express ★ Friday, April 1, 1955

Two Travelogue Pioneers Meet

By DAVID BONGARD

We spent a few minutes the other day with two pioneer factions in the travel film business.

One was the venerable Burton Holmes and the other faction is composed of George Perkins and Lowell F. Wentworth, producers of Filmorama.

Both factions are leaders in the field today, with the latter pursuing new horizons on a wide screen innovation for 16mm travelogues.

Holmes first went into business for paying customers back in Chicago in 1893. He had been lecturing for the fun of it long before that.

In Good Health

The 84-year-old Holmes is the picture of health, we are happy to report. He has a bit of trouble on damp days with his leg which was injured in an auto accident several years ago in Finland.

Holmes' fine wit sparkled as he sat by what he describes as the first swimming pool in Hollywood. The Wistaria covered home once was leased by Francis X. Bushman, and is located in the Hollywood Hills.

"What kind a pose would you like, B. H.? asked Perkins.

"I know nothing about photography. You arrange it," was Holmes' twinkling reply.

Perkins and Wentworth (the latter is the photographer of Filmorama) once were associated with the Holmes producing company. In the past few seasons the pair have made "Four Seasons in New England," "Niagara to Newfoundland" and "Grand Tour of Europe" for the Holmes company.

The wide screen, measuring 32 feet by 18 feet, shows a 16mm Bell and Howell anamorphic lens picture.

Shooting the subject is simple, reports Wentworth, who says that there is no change in choice of subject from the conventional size projection. .

"You just have to be careful

FILMORAMA'S GEORGE PERKINS; BURTON HOLMES
Filmorama's Lowell Wentworth Took the Picture

of your close-ups. We darken the picture o nthe sides and the audience never notices that the full screen is not used," he added.

Lent Lens

Bell and Howell lent them the lens to make tests from November 1953 to May 1954, during which time they photographed every type of outdoor subject under all conditions. From May to July the pair incorporated their company with three other directors.

During the four weeks of incorporation, they also arranged for a bankroll and for transportation to Europe. They sailed in July and remained in Europe shooting the film until December during one of the wettest seasons the continent has experienced.

After Filmorama completes its tour in about a year, the pair are planning to cover Central America.

You may still see the highlights of Europe, with concentration on the Swiss Alps in the latter part of the picture, at the Wilshire Ebell Theater tonight, tomorrow, on Monday and on Wednesday nights.

ROPING A HOG

91

During World War II, meat was in short supply because it was needed for the armed services. My dad bought a farm in Wilmington, Massachusetts, to raise hogs, often called pigs. At that time, garbage was collected from individual families separately from their trash. Nearly all homes had a garbage pail or container. Some were sunk into the ground, and others were above ground but had covers.

In the summer, garbage could become quite ripe in the heat. The garbage was collected by what we loved to call "honey wagons." The garbage was used to feed hogs. Hogs seemed willing to eat almost anything, and the rotting garbage seemed to please the hogs, but a hog farm was not too enjoyable for people in the summer.

When I was fifteen and somewhat dimwitted, I was taught how to use a lasso during my stay with my adopted grandfather at his ranch in Montana. Throwing a lasso and catching a hog required considerable practice. Hogs needed lots of water to help them swallow the garbage. Dad had a brook on his farm, and he put a dam in to back up the running water and preserve it. The brook ran through the feeding area of the hogs and created good old-fashioned mud. Once again, it pleased the happy hogs.

On a day that is embedded forever in my memories, I decided to show Dad and his hired man, who cared for Dad's hogs, how able I had become when I used a lasso. A three-hundred-pound English red hog happened to wander by me at just the wrong moment for him and the right moment for me. I looped my lasso and threw it perfectly over the head of that hog and pulled it tight. That hog took off. Being dimwitted, I had not calculated on how to hold the hog inside the lasso.

A three-hundred-pound hog is very strong and quite fast. In about three steps, I fell flat on my face. Further proof of my lack of a proper plan on how to hold that roped hog was the fact that I had tied my end of the lasso around my waist so I wouldn't drop it. I was now flat on the ground being pulled—head first and at an increasing speed—toward the brook that ran through the feeding area of the hogs.

Suddenly, there was deep, thick mud. Still flat on the ground, I hit the mud head first, and the hog never even slowed down. Then came the garbage feeding area. I was still flat and covered with mud and the leavings of garbage from overfed hogs, only to find myself face first in the garbage, which displeased the other hogs.

My hog came to a corner in the fence and could go no further. He turned to vent his displeasure on what was left of me. A hog's head is shaped a lot like a V. When he turned toward me, the lasso simply fell off. I was beyond being a mess; I was a disaster. I dragged myself out of the hog-feeding area and went to find my dad.

There he was with his hired hand. Sympathy? Hah! One look at me, and there was no way into his automobile with my being covered in garbage. Embarrassment reigned supreme. The cleanup is too agonizing to describe. I got no sympathy even from my mother. She was concerned for the hog!

BEETLES FOR CHRISTMAS

92

We enjoyed our three sons. George was ten years old, Clifton was seven, and Mark was six. My dear wife, Mildred, read about a little playhouse she could buy, all packaged, that we could put together. It had real wood that still had the bark from the trees that was used to make the siding of the little house, and a roof that would allow children to play outside, even in the rain. I was shocked because she bought it!

It arrived eight days before Christmas. It is usually very cold in Massachusetts at that time of year, and there is often snow. Mildred explained to me that she wanted to have her sons enjoy their new playhouse for Christmas. Dutifully, I proceeded, with her "help," to build the playhouse in our living room. I opened the huge package after the boys were in bed and before Santa Claus arrived. We worked all night, and by six o'clock the next morning, the roof was on, and we were done. The boys woke up about 6:10, and all the work was worth it when we saw their disbelieving faces.

But wait! When the boys started playing in the playhouse, there was activity. Beetles! Little and not-so-little, black, fast-moving, hard-shell bugs liked the warm living room, and they became very active. The boys caught dozens over the next two weeks.

Mildred and I were shocked with these "family additions," but the boys made a game of it. None of our family members could believe that we had so much going on in our living room. As soon as the warm weather arrived, we moved the playhouse, the beetles, and our sons outside. That little house lasted for a number of years in our backyard and continues to be a conversation piece.

George, Mark and Clifton before the beetles awaken!

CURRY COLLEGE

93

Trying to talk Mildred Boyle into becoming my wife included attempts spread out over nearly four years. During that period, she wisely refused to marry me three times. I decided to go around her and tried to talk her father into approving, giving her an opportunity to say yes, but he refused, just as she had. Finally, on my knees, I asked that fourth time, and she agreed, much to my delight. However, there was an *if*. She agreed to marry me *if* I finished my college education. She was wise beyond her years.

I needed a year and a half of college credits to receive my bachelor's degree. I was already involved deeply in world-travel motion pictures. A young attorney was a friend; we both lived in Melrose, Massachusetts. Mount Hood was a golf course and winter skiing location in Melrose. While we were playing at Mount Hood, my friend told me that I should look at Curry College in Boston because he had benefited at Curry, where he'd successfully learned to improve his public speaking and lecturing. I realized that was just what I needed and telephoned the president of Curry College the following day.

The president's wife happened to answer my telephone call and set up an appointment to meet the president of the college, Dr. Miller. The end result allowed me to join the classes at Curry held in their headquarters in Boston. The young attorney's advice was beneficial. I was able to transfer all my credits from my three years of completed course work at Northeastern University to Curry. During the next six months, I proved to my wife, Mildred, that I would complete my college education for a bachelor's degree. We were married in 1951.

In 1952, I completed what turned out to be five years of college education and graduated from Curry College in June 1952 with a Bachelor of Science of Oratory Degree. I am happy to report that Mildred enjoyed the degree celebration.

Soon after I graduated, Dr. Miller had the opportunity to obtain a new location for the college (its present location). Dr. and Mrs. Miller had become dear friends, and I was the first person to visit Curry's new location in Milton, Massachusetts, with Dr. Miller. He did not enjoy driving, so I had the privilege of picking him up in Boston and spending the day with him in Milton. For the next months, Dr. Miller and I were together often, primarily because of his dislike of driving. Thanks to the education I received at Curry, I was able to move quickly into the world of creating motion pictures, world travel, and presenting those pictures nationwide.

Working with Dr. Miller in purchasing the college's new campus, with all of the agonies such a huge development brings, was an extraordinary experience. In 1963, Dr. Miller came to see me in my office on State Street in Boston, and he asked me to become a Trustee of my college.

During one three-year period, I brought special classes to the seniors as a visiting professor without salary. I considered the opportunity a privilege. My son, George III, arranged for a Curry group to visit the television production location of "Desperate Housewives" in Hollywood. He was the producer.

The challenge to help move the college forward became a major part of my life. I accepted the trusteeship and served the college as a trustee for forty-two years. I am eager to include the many values the college provided to me in this book. Curry College is an important part of my life.

A LUCKY HANDBAG

94

Mildred's father, Dr. Milton Boyle, joined us on our visit to the macadamia nut showplace in Hawaii. It is a popular location that attracts large numbers of visitors. We parked our automobile and joined a crowd of a couple of hundred other visitors. We enjoyed learning more about Hawaii's famous nut factory and product, while sampling the macadamia nuts. I asked Mildred's dad to wait with her while I went to pick up the car, and Mildred asked him to hold her very heavy handbag while she visited the ladies' room.

I pulled up in front of the door, they both got in, and we took off. We had been traveling for about ten minutes when Mildred asked her Dad for her handbag. There was dead silence for a moment, and then Dad said, "I don't have it. I left it under my seat where I was sitting."

Mildred was in shock! Due to our business meetings, Mildred was carrying her best jewelry in her handbag. The handbag was left under a chair surrounded by a crowd of people. I instantly did a complete turn-around of the car and drove the nine miles to where Dad had been sitting with the crowd. Dad jumped out of the automobile and rushed to the chair he had been using. It is hard to believe, but no one had touched that lonely bag, and Mildred's jewelry was safe—and so now was Dr. Boyle—very relieved and very fortunate!

THE KING RANCH

95

In 1933, my dad read in *Fortune* magazine about the world's biggest ranch, the King Ranch in Texas. We were newly aware of ranches because of our developing friendship with Dick Randall and his OTO Dude Ranch in Montana.

Dad was caught up in marveling that anyone owned millions of acres of ranch land. He often talked about it. Then he read about a King horse, Assault, winning in thoroughbred racing.

In 1946, Dad decided to travel cross-country again. I wrote the King Ranch and asked for an opportunity to visit. It was to be a surprise for my dad, and it worked! We drove to Texas, and I showed him my invitation. We changed direction just a bit and followed my letter of travel directions successfully to the King gate. The ranch had been developed from the year 1824 by a man named Richard King. We spent a day and a night at the ranch.

It would be difficult for us, even in our wildest imaginations, to comprehend the size of the ranch, as well as the research that produced their own breed of horses and cows, which could handle minimal amounts of water and food when other animals failed to survive. My unique feelings were new to me. In that short twenty-four-hour stay at the King, I had a feeling that was a little like a challenge. It seemed to tell me about the value of attitude. I was just twenty.

For Christmas in 1958, A. D. Hall, a distant cousin of my mother, gave me two books on the King Ranch. These books, written by Tom Lea, cover the history of the King family and are wonderful reading.

FILMORAMA ADVENTURE

96

George W. Perkins, a young Boston adventurer and photographer, had been invited in 1950 (when he was but twenty-three years old) to join the staff of the Burton Holmes Travelogues as Associate Narrator. Thus, he got his training under the man, now eighty-five and living in retirement in Hollywood, who invented the word *travelogue* and who is regarded as the greatest master of the strictly travel film. Perkins narrated Burton Holmes Travelogues in Carnegie Hall, New York; in Orchestra Hall, Chicago; and in other leading cities.

In the fall of 1954, just before his season opened, Ray Eggersted, one of the younger stars in the travelogue field, died suddenly of a heart attack. Eggersted was scheduled to give the premiere performance of his new *Vacation in the Alps* for the World Adventure Series in Detroit the following month (October 1954). Perkins jumped into the breach, mastered itinerary script and background music, and gave the Eggersted show a most creditable opening in Detroit.

Meanwhile, Perkins had been pondering the possible use of the new 16 mm wide-angle lens to the travelogue field. The lens had just been invented, and use of it would involve a much greater expense in picture taking. It would also involve transporting from city to city a special portable wide-screen, lens and special projection equipment, capable of developing a vastly larger volume of light, so as to blow up the 16 mm film to double size without loss of brilliance. Special cooling devices would be needed on the projector too, lest the increased heat do damage to the film. Also involved was another limitation. Because of the expense of the production, only large cities with large auditoriums could expect to present it.

The prospect stimulated the Perkins imagination. Eggersted had complained that without a wide-angle 16 mm lens, he could not get the full sweep of Paris' famous Place de la Concorde in one single picture. There were other shots that called for the wide-angle lens, such as the heart of Istanbul, with the busy Galata Bridge across the Golden Horn, and, in the background, the procession of domed and minareted mosques across the horizon. There were the snowcapped mountains of Switzerland, stretched in silhouette across one's vision from aerial gondola but needing a wide-angle lens to capture the full panorama. There was London and the Thames, the Rhine River cruise, Athens and the Acropolis, Rome with its Tiber and Vatican City and Saint Peter's. All these familiar sights—and scores more—could take on a new and startling realism if photographed with the new lens. It was a challenging concept.

To start, Perkins needed three things: (1) ability to use the new lens, (2) the money to produce the travelogue, and (3) associates to help develop the project. With characteristic energy, he attacked this three-headed problem. He obtained the new lens from Bell and Howell and started using it in test productions around Boston. He lined up a small group of farsighted citizens who bought stock in the new enterprise. His associates, too, he chose wisely. One was John Roberts, producer of color movies for the United States Army and for large corporations. For ten years Roberts had produced worldwide pictures for Lowell Thomas. He also chose Lowell Wentworth, his own associate in several noteworthy Burton Holmes productions. Fourth key man in the project was Clayton Ballou, a specialized television producer and film editor.   The four put their heads together.

Meanwhile, the proposed itinerary in Europe took form. The new lens was tested in different parts of the United States—in cities, mountains, and the countryside—under all circumstances and handicaps likely to be encountered in Europe. Finally, the team was confident that it had mastered the photographic problem.

Next, the itinerary. It was decided that *Filmorama Adventure* should include as many of the most famed and favorite tourist places as an evening's entertainment would permit. Selected for filming were the English countryside and London; Amsterdam, Volendam, and Holland; Paris, the French Riviera, and Monte Carlo; complete tours of the Rhineland and Switzerland; Venice, Pisa, Rome, and Vatican City; Athens; and Istanbul.

Two camera crews divided this arduous assignment and worked five months on it. Adding hugely to the expense was the fact that Europe, in the summer of 1954, experienced much rainy weather, and the color camera demands sunshine. In spots, bad weather lasted as many as sixteen days without a break. In London, the crew waited twenty-two days for a half day of bright sunshine. Even Switzerland, where the weather is generally good, frowned on picture taking, with weeks of wet and murky weather. The weeks passed, and the bank account dwindled, but the crews stayed on until the job was complete and fully up to standard. On November 3, the cameramen headed home.

Between November 5 and November 15, four miles of film had to be edited, a complete musical score arranged and recorded, and the New England premiere given. The editing was completed at eleven thirty in the morning on Monday, November 15. Perkins viewed the entire show for the first time that afternoon, and that same evening, he narrated it without script.

"How we made it," Perkins said wearily, "can only be told in terms of nights without sleep and endless hours on the editing and recording tables by our three men in the production department. Without those three men, *Filmorama Adventure* would never have been completed on time. It is doubtful if three men could have been found anywhere in the country who would have worked longer hours or any harder than Lowell Wentworth, John Roberts, and Clayton Ballou."

There was a projection problem too. The portable screen had to be brought in and set up for each performance. The projector, developing two and one-half times the volume of light normally used, was a special job, with special cooling devices. A stagehand crew required three hours just to install and test the equipment.

When *Filmorama Adventure* made its Midwest debut in Chicago's Orchestra Hall the installation crew could not—because of a matinee performance—enter the auditorium until five thirty. The performance was set for a quarter after eight that evening. The screen was still being installed when the early-comers took their seats. Like many success stories, this one ended happily. All performances were sensationally successful.

In Chicago's Orchestra Hall, a packed house paid the largest gross for any travelogue ever presented in the fifty-year history of the hall. In the Boston debut, a capacity house applauded long and loud. When the show was presented in a large New England city, the management immediately rebooked it for three more performances. When *Filmorama Adventure* was announced to a suburban Chicago lecture audience as an extra attraction, every seat was subscribed for in twelve minutes.

It is predicted that the new wide-angle lens will revolutionize the color-movie travelogue field. The picture below is of the installation for the commemoration exercises at Besser Manufacturing Plant, Alpena, Michigan. The 33 foot portable screen is installed on a 10-ton crane for top suspension. The screen, one of the largest portable screens in the world is used by the Colonial Pictures Co. of Lynnfield Center, Massachusetts for special presentations of the 16mm color motion picture, Filmorama.

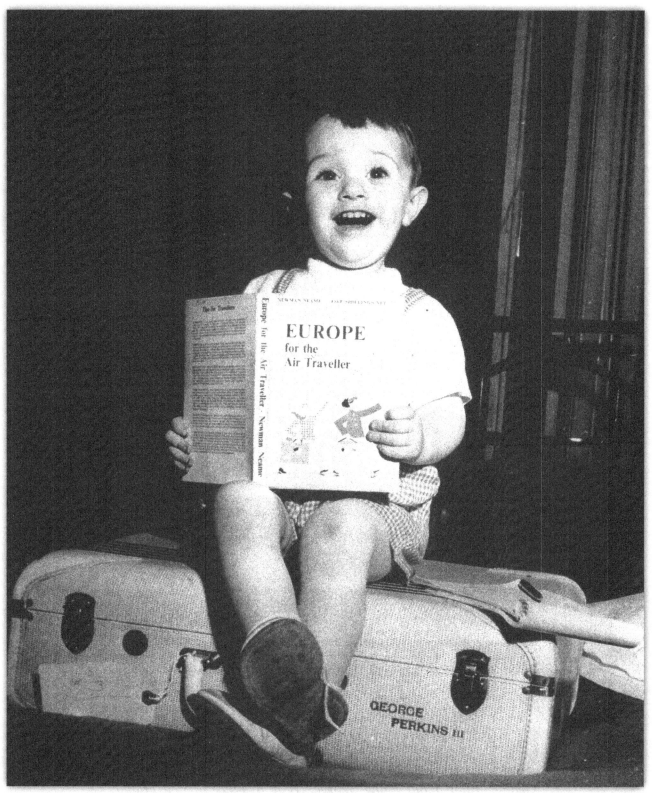

George, III Packed to Travel

Screen being set up on the crane for the show

George, Mildred and young George, III at breakfast in Switzerland.

Lowell Wentworth, color film expert at work.

HIGHLIGHTS OF EUROPE

Through the 16mm.
FilmoRama Wide Screen
Lens for the first time!

SWITZERLAND

Lake Lucerne
St. Moritz
Matterhorn
Jungfrau
Geneva
Alpine atmosphere

FILMORAMA

FRANCE

Paris
Versailles
People of France
Rural France
Riviera
Chateaus of old

FILMORAMA

GERMANY

Cologne
Romantic Rhine
Castle days
Frankfurt
Heidelberg
Black Forest

FILMORAMA

ITALY

Venice
Lake Regions
Florence
Rome
Naples
Capri
Italian Riviera

FILMORAMA

—and others:

ENGLAND
HOLLAND
BELGIUM
AUSTRIA
SPAIN
PORTUGAL
TURKEY

FILMORAMA

EXCLUSIVE AGENTS
IN U. S. and CANADA

National Lecture Bureau, Inc.

FORD HICKS, Manager

541 Diversey Parkway · Chicago 14, Illinois
Telephone GRaceland 2-2872

*The World is Yours
Through FilmoRama!*

Sold out audience

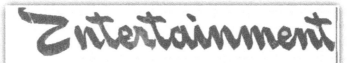

Entertainment

14   CITIZEN NEWS   ✦   Tuesday March 15 1955

'Filmorama' Spectacle Awes Audience at Wilshire Ebell

By BRANC COREY

Another f rst was sc ed at the W lsh re Ebell Theater last n ght when the west coast debut of F lmoram a was presented bef re an enthus ast c packed house Th s marked the f rst show hg of 16 mm travel f lm on a w de screen Done n color the f lm Highl ghts of E rope prov ded as beaut ful and spec tacula a f lm as has been seen locally m qu te a wb le The show ng w ll be repeated Thurs day even ng

H ghl ghts of Europe s just that Ge rge Perk ns pl otog rapher and narrator of the f lm can r gh ly be cred ted w th l ft ing the 16mm travel g e nts the spectacle echelon for n F lmorama he has ach eved w dth photog apl c excellence and a mus c score of outstand ng mer t

Most of the aud ence has been well nformed on the age old beaut f E rope The color f the Se ne R ver as t v nds t self through t e br ll ant patch work f c v l zat n vh ch s Par s and wh ch s F ance t self They have heard of the fabul us resplendency wl ch s the Med terranean Sea lapp ng aga nst the R viera In the travelogue th s much heralded beaut s truly underscored Germany w th ts great P lack Forest ts unco l ng Rh ne R ver Frankfurt Berl n and the my r ad of v llages and t wns crest ing the r chness of ts country s de are portrayed throu h a lens w th an nherent warmth for color l ondon the Mall P cad l ly C rcus and the f sherme on the T ames are all very much al ve w th a color and deep hued mpress on sm wh ch s a joy to behold And from Europe s op pos te s des the unend ng mag c of her s scrut n zed and caressed

by the lens of George Perk ns Truly a well done product on

For the h stor cally m nded there w ll be pleasu e in the rem nants of Rome s anc ent c v l za t on and the Greek ru ns For the m nds of the contemporar es amusement m the many Coca Cola and Texaco gas l ne ad vertisements wh ch glut the great App an Way the march route of h stor s Emperor Cae sar And for e err ne seeing F lmorama there w ll be an even ng extremely well spent

EPILOGUE

The 6th day of October is welcomed as the completion of another happy year that Mildred and I have been together. The Concord's Colonial Inn in Concord, Massachusetts is the oldest continually operating Inn in the United States. When we married on October 6, 1951 we chose it for our wedding night.

Every year on our anniversary we have dinner at the Inn as it holds a special place in our hearts. Saturday night, October 6, 2018, was no different. We arrived in our Subaru and I let Mildred out at the door. I spent the next twenty minutes trying to locate a parking place as there was another celebration going on and the place was packed. Finally, I parked the car and went in to find Mildred. She was in the waiting room enjoying the company of two people from New York who were staying there. The man greeted me with a warm smile and commented on the reason we were there and as a happy couple married for 67 years. They were Greg and Camille Harlow and we enjoyed our few moments together immensely.

We were called to the dining room, as our reservation was ready. It is a beautiful large room with lovely furnishings and decorations, reminding us of its famous past. After experiencing the perfect location, atmosphere, quality of food, and the fine service of our server, Bill, it was time to ask for the check. According to Bill, there was no charge. Shock! How could that be? He stated that the dinners were all paid for, but he was not allowed to tell us by whom. I asked him to let me provide the tip, but he declined, saying that he had been more than adequately tipped for his service.

Mildred and I were amazed. Mildred asked if it could have been the friendly couple from New York. I tried for nearly an hour to obtain help in locating the "who". I was able to find out that there were four couples from New York staying at the Inn that night, so I wrote four "thank you" notes and asked the front desk to put one in each of their boxes. That way I would be able to acknowledge my appreciation.

On the way to our car, we ran into our two new friends. We got them to admit to their generous gift. What a privilege it is to meet unique, happy people like them. They belong in the book, as they are "special people".

One final note. The last two photographs on the next page are to me what life is about – connecting with people from all walks of life and making new friends. On one of our many travels across the country we came across a man on a horse carrying a coyote pup. My mother, Daisy, took a picture of him with a box camera. She mailed him that photo and a great many days later she received this note from him. There it is, a connection and a new friend.

JE Graham

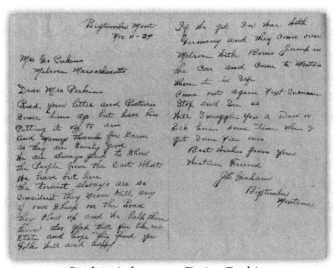

Graham's letter to Daisy Perkins

SOME OF THE PEOPLE WHO GAVE MY LIFE ITS VALUES

Mildred, my wife – *EVERYTHING*, including her trust in me when we were apart

My dad and my mother – *ETHICS*, honesty, belief in hard work, gifting and *LOVE*

Mildred's mother and dad – *BACKUP* in our marriage, especially her mother Etta

Frederick Snyder – kindness, *THOUGHTFULNESS*, greatness, *NEVER GIVE UP*

Dow Hicks – kindness, *HONESTY*, hard work, successful image

Jack Bowen – *TRUST*, kindness, *FRIENDSHIP*

Dick Randall – let me call him *GRAMP*, *TRUE MEANING OF A HANDSHAKE*, think how to make a task easier before doing it, long term friendship

Frances Mont – how to take orders, be a working member, *PRACTICE*

Rhetta Wilson – how to make a partnership work and *DO YOUR HARD WORK* well

Bess Erskine – how to handle a horse, friendship for a lifetime, *NEVER FORGET* a favor done

Burton Holmes – gift of enormous advantage in chosen field, being kind, *PATIENCE AND CONTROL* under major duress, personal appearance

Lowell Wentworth – *MY BEST MAN*, I became his best man, *TRAVEL PARTNER*, great camera skills, understanding when needed, control under great stress, never give up

Robert Pitcher – a great leader, an understanding and patient *BOSS*, a man I would like to be

Judge Byron Elliott – a *KEEPER OF PROMISES*, a guide in life, remarkable and good friend

Clyde Erskine – Bess Randall's husband, an engineer and executive, *FAMILY* above all else

Bill Randall – guide, rancher, tough, able, made you think of *WHAT NOT TO BE*

Walter Bonin – associate, *FRIEND BEYOND BELIEF*, business angle, total *DEVOTION* to his wife

Bob Dow – *LIFETIME FRIEND*, partner in Renault road test, MIT engineer, successful

Dorothy Reed – my *FIRST GIRLFRIEND* at age 12. My first real girlfriend at age 16, separated by World War 2, still friends at 87. She was 5 months older than I am

Shirley Ann Singleton – we met by accident while I was in the Navy and on a ship. She was a model in Boston. We met by letter. After a few dates we agreed on a brother and sister relationship. It lasted until her death 61 years later. Her children are also my friends. *FRIENDSHIP is a BLESSED human value.*

And so many others.

THE WRINKLES ON THE FACE OF LIFE
George William Perkins, II

When I look in my mirror
At the wrinkles that showed
Some had come from laughter
Some had come from woes
Life offers the opportunity
To reap what you sow
I have tried to be certain
Laughter out did the woe

LOVE FAMILY FREINDSHIP

ACKNOWLEDGEMENTS

Mildred Perkins
George W. Perkins, III
Clifton Alfred Dow Perkins
Mark Paige Perkins
Ron Hudson
Judy Ranan
Douglas Brown, Groton School
Major Richard Henry Randall
Nanci Anderson
D.N.H.
ADVANCED PHOTO

Daisy   *George, II*   *George, Sr.*

Printed in the United States
By Bookmasters